EXAM ESSENTIALS PRAC

D0537221

IELTS 1

Mark Harrison
Russell Whitehead

NATIONAL GEOGRAPHIC LEARNING | CENGAGE Learning

Australia • Brazil • Japan • Korea • Mexico • Singapore • Spain • United Kingdom • United States

Exam Essentials Practice Tests 1
IELTS

Mark Harrison and Russell Whitehead

Publisher: Gavin McLean

Publishing Consultant: Karen Spiller

Editorial Project Manager: Stephanie Parker

Development Editor: Deborah Chagal Friedland

Content Project Managers: Tom Relf and Amy Borthwick

Marketing Manager: Charlotte Ellis

Manufacturing Buyer: Eyvett Davis

Cover design: Oliver Hutton

Compositor: Cenveo® Publisher Services

National Geographic Liaison: Wesley Della Volla

DVD-ROM: Tom, Dick and Debbie Ltd

Contributing writers:
Alison Ramage (video materials)
Carole Allsop, Sarah Emsden-Bonfanti,
Margaret Matthews (new texts)

ISBN (with key): 978-1-285-74719-4
ISBN (without key): 978-1-285-74721-7

National Geographic Learning
Cheriton House, North Way, Andover, Hampshire, SP10 5BE
United Kingdom

Cengage Learning is a leading provider of customised learning solutions with office locations around the globe, including Singapore, the United Kingdom, Australia, Mexico, Brazil and Japan. Locate our local office at
international.cengage.com/region

Cengage Learning products are represented in Canada by Nelson Education Ltd.

Visit National Geographic Learning online at **ngl.cengage.com**
Visit our corporate website at **www.cengage.com**

CREDITS
Although every effort has been made to contact copyright holders before publication, this has not always been possible. If notified, the publisher will undertake to rectify any errors or omissions at the earliest opportunity.

Texts:
The publishers would like to thank the following for permission to use copyright material:

Page 33: Adapted from 'It takes more than a good degree to be a good teacher' by Francis Gilbert, *The Guardian*, 19.1.10, Copyright Guardian News & Media Ltd 2010. Page 38: From 'The Birth of Our Modern Minds' by Roger Highfield, *The Telegraph*, 15.10.03, © Telegraph Media Group Ltd 2003. Page 44: Charts from 'A Regional Language Revival, Part 1: France' by Anne Judge, *The Linguist*, Vol. 41, October-November 2003. Copyright © 1999 Anne Judge. Page 66: From *The Longman History of the United States of America*, Brogan, H. (1990), Copyright © 1990 Pearson Education Ltd. Page 72: From 'How bugs hitch-hike across the galaxy' by David Derbyshire, *The Telegraph*, 5.11.03, © Telegraph Media Group Ltd 2003. Page 78: From 'Finding out about the world from television news' by David Morley in *Television and Common Knowledge*, Gripsrud, J. (ed). Copyright © 1999 Routledge. Reproduced by permission of Taylor & Francis Books UK. Page 84: Table from 'The Sunday Times 50 best small companies to work for', *Sunday Times*, © News Syndication, 2004. Page 96: From 'Working in the Movies' by Melanie Leyshon, *ITI Bulletin*, May-June 2003. Reproduced with kind permission from the Institute of Translation & Interpreting and the author. Page 100: From 'Hands-on healing, or a con?' by Orla Kennedy, *The Telegraph*, 10.9.03, © Telegraph Media Group Ltd 2003. Page 105: Adapted from 'Path of the Jaguar' by Mel White, http://ngm.nationalgeographic.com/2009/03/jaguars/white-text, March 2009. Page 116: From *Groucho Marx and Other Short Stories* by Robert Bader. Excerpt Used by Permission. Collection, Introductions, Editor's Note, Notes and Chronology © 1993 and 2011 by Robert Bader. Special thanks to Applause Books. Page 120: From 'Molehills made out of mountains' by Anna Grayson, *The Telegraph*, 17.9.01, © Telegraph Media Group Ltd 2001. Page 124: From 'Think happy' by John Elliott, *The Sunday Times*, © John Elliott, News Syndication, 2003. Page 128: From *Local Heroes: Do-It-Yourself Science* by Adam Hart-Davis and Paul Bader. Published by BBC Books. Reprinted by permission of The Random House Group Limited. Page 136: Adapted from 'Do birds smell?' by Tim Birkhead, *Bird Table*, Spring 2012. Page 141: From *Personality Assessment*, Vernon, P.E., Copyright © 1964 Routledge. Reproduced by permission of Taylor & Francis Books UK. Page 144: From TITAN of Technology, first published in CAM, the University of Cambridge Alumni Magazine. Page 148: Figures from *The Londoner*, February 2004. Page 156: From 'How to run a ...' by David Harvey, *The Author*, Summer 2003, © David Harvey 2003. Page 161: Adapted from 'Modernism: a concrete utopia' by Lara Fiegel, *The Guardian*, 1.9.11, Copyright Guardian News & Media Ltd 2011. Page 164: Adapted from 'How the visual language of comics could have its roots in the ice age' by David Robson, *The Observer*, 24.11.13, Copyright Guardian News & Media Ltd 2013. Page 173: Adapted from 'Look before you leap into an suitable place to live' by Fred Redwood, *The Times*, 24.8.00, © Fred Redwood, News Syndication, 2003. Page 175: Adapted from 'The best summer festivals of 2013' by Natalie Paris, http://www.telegraph.co.uk/travel/festivalsandevents/10015516/The-best-summer-festivals-of-2013 .html, 24.4.13, © Telegraph Media Group Ltd 2013. Page 181: From 'To my horror, I couldn't even write' by Christine Doyle, *The Telegraph*, 2003, © Telegraph Media Group Ltd 2003. Page 187: From *Walk for Life*, *Walkers News*. Contains public sector information licensed under the Open Government Licence v1.0. Page 189: Adapted from 'New York on a budget', http://www.telegraph .co.uk/travel/destinations/northamerica/usa/newyork/9570093/New-York-on-a-budget-the-best-cheap-hotels-and-restaurants.html, 27/9/12, © Telegraph Media Group Ltd 2012. Page 194: From 'Natural assets worth saving in the outback' by John Craven, *The Mail on Sunday*, 28.6.10. Page 207: IELTS Listening and Reading answer sheets. Reproduced with permission of Cambridge English Language Assessment ©UCLES 2014.

Printed in China by RR Donnelley
1 2 3 4 5 6 7 8 9 10 – 18 17 16 15 14

Contents

Exam Essentials is a series of materials for students preparing for the major EFL/ESL examinations, such as Cambridge English: First (FCE), Cambridge English: Advanced (CAE), Certificate of Proficiency in English (CPE), and International English Language Testing System (IELTS), Each book in the series pays close attention to developing a detailed knowledge of the skills and strategies needed for success in each part or paper of the exams.

IELTS Practice Tests helps learners become aware of IELTS exam requirements, offers details about the format of the exam and helps learners develop the exam skills necessary for success. The book also offers extensive practice in all parts of the exam, using the actual test format. As well as students who are planning to take the IELTS exam, the book is also suitable for use by teachers of IELTS courses and by students and teachers involved in checking and improving academic English.

1 Taking the IELTS Exam

The IELTS exam, which is jointly managed by the University of Cambridge ESOL Examinations (Cambridge ESOL), the British Council and IDP: IELTS Australia, assesses the language ability of candidates who need to study or work where English is the language of communication. IELTS is recognised by universities and employers in many countries, such as Australia, Canada, New Zealand, the UK and the USA, as well as by professional bodies, immigration authorities and other government agencies.

There are four parts to the IELTS exam: Listening, Reading, Writing and Speaking. All candidates take the same Listening and Speaking Modules, while the Reading and Writing Modules are available in two formats – Academic and General Training.

The Academic Reading and Writing Modules assess whether a candidate is ready to study or train in the medium of English. The General Training Modules focus on basic survival skills in a broad social and educational context, and are more suitable for candidates who are going to English-speaking countries for the purposes of work experience, non-degree level training or immigration.

A full breakdown of the format, task types and timing of each Module can be found on the inside front cover of this *Practice Test* book.

IELTS candidates receive a Band Score from 1 to 9 for each Module of the test, and an Overall Band Score from 1 to 9, which is an average of the four Module scores.

One mark is awarded for each correct answer in the Listening and Reading Modules. A confidential Band Score conversion table is then used to translate these total marks into IELTS band scores. Scores are reported as a whole Band or a half Band.

Writing tasks are assessed independently by certified IELTS examiners, according to the 9-Band scale. Writing scripts are assessed on the following criteria:

Task achievement/response
Task 1: Has the writer included all the relevant information?
Task 2: Has the writer fully answered the question by dealing with all parts of it?

Coherence and cohesion
Does the answer flow well and is there a clear progression of information and opinions with appropriate linking words and phrases?

Lexical resource: Has the writer used appropriate vocabulary? Is the vocabulary accurately used?

Grammatical range and accuracy: Has the writer used a good level of grammatical structures and linking words and phrases? Is the grammar used accurate and not too simple?

For information on the criteria used for assessing the Speaking Module, see page 88.

Further information about the exam can also be obtained from the IELTS website: **www.ielts.org**

2 *IELTS Practice Tests*: contents

IELTS Practice Tests prepares candidates for the IELTS examination by providing **six full practice tests**, which follow the latest exam specifications.

There are **two guided tests**, which provide clear, authoritative and complete guidance on the task types featured in each section of the exam.

These guided tests are followed by **four tests (without guidance)**, which offer students thorough practice at a realistic exam level.

An additional **General Training section** contains the Reading and Writing Modules for two practice tests.

Together, these tests provide at least two opportunities to practise every task type, whilst covering as full a range as possible of typical IELTS topic areas and situations.

The DVD-ROM accompanying the book include the **audio materials** for the Listening Modules, recorded so as to reflect accurately the audio element of the actual exam. The DVD-ROM also contains a full model Speaking interview. For more details see the DVD-ROM introduction on the inside back cover.

A **writing bank** has sample answers for the writing tasks, for both Academic and General Training tests.

IELTS Practice Tests with key edition contains a comprehensive **answer key**, which includes detailed explanations of each answer for the Listening and Reading Modules, and an **annotated audio script**.

Sample exam answer sheets on pages 207–208 can be photocopied and used to give you practice of what you will have to do in the exam.

3 How to use *IELTS Practice Tests*

Students:
You can use this book in different ways, according to your needs: your level, your aims, how much time you have, if you are studying completely by yourself or with a class and teacher.

IELTS uses many task types and you need to be well prepared for them all in order to do well in the exam. *IELTS Practice Tests* will help you to do this.

Use the Exam overview to understand the overall content and format of the test. Look through Test 3 to see how the description in the chart matches the test.

Teachers:
Remember that IELTS is not like an exam that has a specific syllabus that it will test. Your skills will be needed to diagnose and address your students' needs in terms of lexis, structure, discourse, and so on. Because *IELTS Practice Tests* covers the full range of exam tasks and a comprehensive range of typical IELTS exam topics, it can help you to concentrate on the linguistic aspects of the course you teach.

Tests 1 and 2

Students:
Tests 1 and 2 contain valuable help in preparing for the exam. All the exam task types are represented and they are clearly headed for easy reference.

For each task, there is a **Task guide**, which gives you important facts and advice for that particular task type.

There is also a **Step-by-step guide** for each task type, which takes you through a series of carefully designed steps that will help you understand how to approach doing the task.

Model answers (on pages 199–206) are provided for all the writing tasks.

One way to use Tests 1 and 2 is to work your way through both tests. This will help you become well informed about what the IELTS exam involves. Alternatively, use Tests 1 and 2 as a sort of reference tool. Practise taking other tests in the book and use Tests 1 and 2 to get advice on particular task types.

Teachers:
This part of the **IELTS Exam Essentials** series could constitute the basis of a short intensive IELTS preparation course. It is also a useful place to check details of particular task types. The exercises and model answers can also be used as the starting points for skills classes.

Tests 3–6

Students:
These four complete tests can be used in a variety of ways. For example, you may:

* work through Tests 1 and 2 first, and use Tests 3–6 to practise what you have studied or

* begin with Tests 3–6, and when you come to each task type, check the task guides in Tests 1 and 2 to make sure you understand how to approach it.

You can use the Tests to create a self-study course:

* Work your way through Tests 1 and 2.

* Do Tests 3 and 4, returning to the task guides in Tests 1 and 2 to prepare yourself for each task type.

* Check your answers carefully – including the audio scripts for the listening sections – and keep notes about the areas where you have problems.

* Do Test 5, while checking your notes; when you reach a task type where you have had a problem before, review the task guides for Tests 1 and 2.

* Take Test 6 under test conditions (correct timing, silence, no dictionaries or reference books, etc.).

When you get an answer wrong, check to see which of the following happened:

* Did you mishear a word in the Listening?

* Did you read the question too quickly and not understand what to look for in the Reading?

* Did you make the wrong interpretation of what the graph represents in the Writing?

* Did you misunderstand what a word or phrase means?

Every question you get wrong is an opportunity to learn something that will help you later in the exam.

Teachers:
You can use the above steps with your students, either in-class or as a structured self-study programme. Encourage your students to build their understanding of the test with the explanatory key and to develop their ability to evaluate their own language and learning needs.

Mark Harrison and Russell Whitehead

▶ **Questions 1–10**

Questions 1–4

Complete the notes below.

Write **NO MORE THAN TWO WORDS AND/OR A NUMBER** *for each answer.*

Easylet Accommodation Agency

Cheapest properties: £ **1** .... per week

Minimum period of contract: **2** ....

Office open Saturdays until **3** ....

List of properties available on **4** ....

Notes completion

Task guide

▶ This task requires you to write answers that are pieces of information given in the recording you hear.

▶ Read the instructions carefully. These will tell you the maximum number of words you can use to answer the questions – this may be as many as three, but may be only two or one. They may also tell you that numbers are required.

▶ The words or numbers you need are on the recording. Do not rephrase or change the form of the words on the recording.

▶ The questions follow the order of the recording.

Step-by-step guide

▶ **Step 1 – Think first**

Look at the notes. What sort of information is required in each gap?

Decide if each gap 1–4 will require: **A** word(s), **B** a number or **C** word(s) and a number.

▶ **Step 2 – Now listen and do the task**

▶ **Step 3 – Check what you heard**

Three things are important: (a) you must be ready for the information, (b) you must write the correct information, and (c) you must be careful not to write the wrong information.

Look at the audio script for *Question 1*. For (a), the words which lead you to the answer are underlined. For (b), the number you must write for the answer is circled. For (c), words which you might wrongly think could be the answer are in *italics*.

Audio script

Man: Easylet. Good morning. How can I help you?
Woman: Hello. I saw your advertisement in the paper and I'm calling to ask about renting a flat.

Man: Certainly. What kind of flat had you in mind?
Woman: Well, er, I don't know exactly ... I mean, it depends on price, to some extent.
Man: OK, now we have properties across the whole range. *The average is probably £120 a week.*
Woman: Oh, I was hoping for something a little cheaper.
Man: They start at £90, that's the lowest we have usually. And *they go up to £200.*
Woman: I could manage the lowest figure.

Now look at the audio script for *Question 2*. Underline the words that lead you to the answer and circle the correct answer.

Audio script

Man: An important question is how long you're thinking of staying in the property. We don't do short lets.
Woman: I'd want a flat for nine months, perhaps longer.
Man: That would be fine. Our contracts are for a standard six months, and that can be extended.
Woman: Fine. I'd need to come in and see you?

Questions 5–7

Choose **THREE** *letters* **A–G**.

Which **THREE** *things are included for free with every property for rent from Easylet?*

5 ....

6 ....

7 ....

A heating bills
B kitchen equipment
C plates and glasses
D sheets and towels
E telephone
F television
G water bill

Multiple-choice with multiple answers (1)

Task guide

- This task requires you to choose correct answers from a list of possible answers.

- You get one mark for each correct answer.

- It's very important to read the instructions carefully. They will tell you what to listen for. You will probably hear something connected with all the options. The instructions will tell you the reason for choosing some of the options on the list.

- The options are usually listed in alphabetical order.

- The order of the options in the list will probably differ from the order of the recording.

- You may hear exactly the same words as appear in the options, or you may hear alternative phrases that have the same meaning.

- You can write the correct answers in any order.

- See also pages 10 and 16 for other types of multiple-choice tasks.

Step-by-step guide

▸ **Step 1 – Think first**

Look at the instructions. You are listening for things that are 'included for free' in 'every property for rent'.

Think about ways of giving this information.

▸ **Step 2 – Check what you will hear**

Look at this part of the audio script, which relates to options B and C.

Audio script

Man: That depends on the flat, to a certain extent, although some things are standard in all flats. For example, **every flat has kitchen equipment provided for your use**. **Woman:** Good. *Does that also mean tableware, cups, glasses, plates?* **Man:** *In some flats, but not all.*

B is a correct answer. C is not a correct answer, although it is clearly mentioned. Plates and glasses are 'included for free', but not in 'every flat'.

▸ **Step 3 – Listen and do the task**

Questions 8–10

Label the map below.

Write the correct letter **A–H** *next to questions 8–10.*

Where are the following blocks of flats situated?

8   Eastern Towers ....

9   Granby Mansions ....

10 Busby Garden ....

Labelling a map/plan/diagram (1)

Task guide

▸ This task requires you to label a map with the correct places or points using the information you hear in the recording. Similar tasks may require you to label a plan or a diagram.

▸ The questions follow the order of the recording. If you realise you have missed one question, make sure you focus carefully for the next one.

▸ The map and the recording will give you a starting point. Listen carefully because finding the answers greatly depends on locating the starting point in the map.

▸ There are several more possible places than you need marked on the map. Follow the speaker's directions carefully before you decide which is the correct place.

▸ The information about the starting point is repeated for each question. Do not worry too much if you miss one question, or feel you have got one question wrong.

▸ See also pages 14 and 64 for other types of labelling tasks.

Step-by-step guide

▸ **Step 1 – Think first**

Look at the map and try to locate the starting point.

Remind yourself of the language of directions: turn left, go straight on, follow along, etc.

The possible places on the map will often be quite close together, so you need to listen carefully to decide which of two or three possibilities is correct in each case.

▸ **Step 2 – Locate the starting point**

Look at this section of the audio script, which tells you where the starting point is, and locate it in the map.

Audio script

Woman: Could you tell me where they are? I'm **at the train station** at the moment.
Man: Eastern Towers, if you're coming **from the station**, isn't very far.

In this case, you should start reading the map in the top left corner, which is clearly marked 'From train station'. This is your starting point for all three blocks of flats.

▸ **Step 3 – Check what you will hear**

Look at the next section of the script. Follow the speaker's directions carefully. Pay special attention to the different references to 'left' and 'right'.

Audio script

Man: Eastern Towers, if you're coming **from the station**, isn't very far. **Cross over** City Bridge. Then **go left**, and where the road divides, you want the **right-hand fork**. You'll see Eastern Towers **on the left side** of the road. It's a lovely building, with trees around it.

The relevant information is in bold. Notice that the reference to trees will not help you find the answer.

▸ **Step 4 – Listen and do the task**

▸ **Questions 11–20**

Questions 11 and 12

For each question, choose **TWO** *letters* **A–E**.

11 Which **TWO** activities for school groups need to be booked one week in advance?
  A drama workshops
  B garden sculpture experience
  C painting demonstrations
  D tours for the blind
  E video making

12 Which **TWO** facilities are closed in winter?
  A adventure playground
  B artists' studio
  C café
  D mini zoo
  E shop

Multiple-choice with multiple answers (2)

Task guide

▸ This task requires you to answer each question by choosing two correct options.

▸ In order to receive one mark for these questions, you need to choose both correct options. There is no half mark for choosing only one correctly.

▸ The length of the recording that you hear in this type of task will be less than when there is one mark for each correct answer (see page 7).

▸ You will probably hear some reference to each of the options on the list. It is, therefore, important that you are clear what you are listening for. Only two of the options will be the correct answers to the question.

▸ The options are usually listed alphabetically. The options don't follow the order in which you will hear the information on the recording.

▸ Make sure you read the list of possible answers very carefully; they are often quite similar.

▸ See also pages 7 and 16 for other types of multiple-choice tasks.

Step-by-step guide

▶ **Step 1 – Think first**

The words on the recording may or may not be the same as the words in the options. Prepare yourself for hearing various ways of describing the options on the list.

For example, option A is 'drama workshops'. You may hear 'drama workshops', but you may also hear 'workshops involving drama', 'practical activities using drama', 'activities that involve acting', and so on.

If you prepare yourself like this, you will be more likely to understand whether option A is a correct answer to *Question 11*.

▶ **Step 2 – Check what you will hear**

Look at options C and D in *Question 11*. Can you think of different ways to describe them?

C painting demonstration: ....

D tours for the blind: ....

Now look at this part of the audio script. Underline the words that relate to options C and D. Are the words used in the audio script the same as in the options? Are they similar to words you predicted?

Audio script

It's nice to see so many of you here. I'm going to tell you something about Hollylands – our facilities and activities, and the exhibitions we have coming up. I hope you'll find it interesting and bring your pupils along. For most of what we have to offer here, you can just turn up with your party. I'm pleased to say that recent work has meant that the whole centre is prepared for blind visitors. There are a couple of activities where we ask you to book a week in advance. We only have artists that you can watch painting at certain times, so we need notice of your coming for that.

▶ **Step 3 – Think about what you hear**

Option C: Blind visitors are mentioned, but there do not seem to be tours for the blind, and there is no requirement to book a certain number of days in advance. Although you hear something about blind people, you do not hear the answer to the question. You should not choose option C as an answer.

Option D: In this case, 'painting demonstrations' has become 'artists that you can watch painting'. You hear that because Hollylands only has 'artists … at certain times' they 'need notice'. This 'notice' links to the previous sentence: 'activities where we ask you to book a week in advance'.

You hear something about options C and D, but only D is a correct answer to *Question 11*.

▶ **Step 4 – Listen and do the task**

LISTENING MODULE	READING MODULE	WRITING MODULE	SPEAKING MODULE

SECTION 1
SECTION 2
SECTION 3
SECTION 4

Questions 13–17

Complete the table below.

Write **NO MORE THAN THREE WORDS AND/OR A NUMBER** *for each answer.*

HOLLYLANDS MUSEUM & EDUCATION CENTRE

EXHIBITION	STARTING DATE	POINTS TO REMEMBER
History in Pictures	13	opportunity to go on an old bus
14	19th September	visitors can use 15 .... service
16	11th November	competition – prize: 17 .... for two people

Table completion

Task guide

▶ This task requires you to listen and fill in a table with the correct information.

▶ It is important to write in exactly what is required, so you should look carefully at the whole table to see how the information is organised.

▶ If there are words or numbers before and/or after the numbered gaps, these are likely not to be the actual words that you hear on the recording, but similar words that have the same meaning.

▶ You must fill in the numbered gaps with the exact words and numbers that you hear on the recording.

▶ Read the instructions carefully. Notice how many words you can use to fill in each gap. The number of words may vary; you may be asked to write a maximum of one, two or three words in each gap. The instructions will also tell you if you need to use a number for your answer.

▶ You need to listen carefully, as the recording may contain other information which may seem correct, but which will in fact be wrong for the purposes of completing the table.

▶ See also page 54 for another type of table completion task.

Step-by-step guide

▸ **Step 1 – Think first**

Prepare for this task by thinking about how the information might be presented on the recording.

For example, an 'exhibition' might be described as a 'show' or an 'event'. These exhibitions might 'have the name', 'have the title' or 'be called' something.

Think of different ways to talk about the 'starting date'.

Starting date: ....

▸ **Step 2 – Check what you will hear**

Look at the audio script for *Question 13*.

Audio script

OK, now we run a programme of exhibitions through the year, so I'll tell you about the next few. Our current exhibition, *Local Lives*, ends on 26th August, and then one called *History in Pictures* starts on 28th August. This includes all sorts of objects and experiences from the past, such as farm machinery and some cars. We're sure children will love the chance to have a ride on an old bus.

1 What is the correct answer for *Question 13*?

....

2 What wrong answer might you write for *Question 13* if you didn't listen carefully?

....

3 How is the 'opportunity to go on an old bus' described on the recording?

....

4 Why should you not write 'on' as part of your answer to *Question 13*?

....

▸ **Step 3 – Listen and do the task**

SECTION 1
SECTION 2
SECTION 3
SECTION 4

Questions 18–20

Label the plan below.

Choose **THREE** *answers from the box and write the letters* **A–F** *next to questions 18–20.*

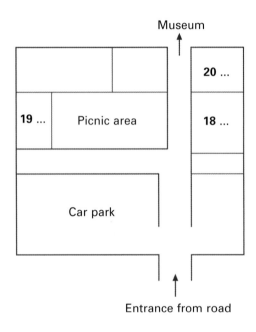

A	bicycle parking
B	drinks machine
C	first aid room
D	manager's office
E	telephones
F	ticket office
G	toilets

18 ....

19 ....

20 ....

Labelling a map/plan/diagram (2) (with choices)

Task guide

▶ This task requires you to label a plan (or map or diagram) correctly.

▶ You must use the information you hear on the recording to decide which of the possible answers are correct for the places marked on the plan.

▶ You may have to find two or more places from a list of several possible answers.

▶ It is important that you look carefully at the plan, so that you are ready to find your way around it while listening to the recording.

▶ The options will probably be listed alphabetically, but the order in which you hear them will probably be different.

▶ If you miss one answer, don't worry too much – move on to the next one. You should be able to find each answer independently of the other(s).

▶ See also pages 8 and 64 for other types of labelling tasks.

Step-by-step guide

▶ **Step 1 – Locate the starting point**

In order to answer the questions correctly, you need to start reading the plan from the correct point. You need to locate the starting point on the plan.

On the plan here, there are two possible starting points: 'Entrance from road' and 'Museum'. Think about the position of the arrows as well. Where will the directions probably start?

▶ **Step 2 – Think first**

It is possible that the options will be expressed in a different way on the recording. Look at how option A is described in the audio script.

Audio script

So, whether you come by car or bicycle, you'll come in from the road. Cars then park to the left, through the gates into the car park, and bikes to the right, through the gates opposite.

1 Is option A a correct answer for *Question 18, 19* or *20*? ....

Now look at how option B is described in the audio script.

Audio script

Cyclists in particular might be feeling thirsty at this point, and you can get a drink from the machine at the end of the bike park, half-way to the museum entrance.

2 Is option B a correct answer for *Question 18, 19* or *20*? ....

3 Options A and B have come first and second in the recording. Do we know if option C will come next? ....

▶ **Step 3 – Listen and do the task**

SECTION 1
SECTION 2
SECTION 3
SECTION 4

▶ **Questions 21–30**

Questions 21–25

Choose the correct letter, **A, B** *or* **C**.

21 Before giving her presentation, Kate was worried about
   A being asked difficult questions.
   B using the projection equipment.
   C explaining statistical results.

22 During many presentations by students, Martin feels that
   A the discussion of research methods is not detailed enough.
   B lecturers do not show enough interest in their students' work.
   C the student does not make enough eye contact with the audience.

23 What is Kate's opinion of the tutorials she attends?
   A They involve too much preparation.
   B They should be held more frequently.
   C They do not have a clear focus.

24 What does Martin intend to do next semester?
   A Make better use of the internet.
   B Improve his note-taking skills.
   C Prioritise reading lists effectively.

25 What problem do Kate and Martin both have when using the library?
   A The opening hours are too short.
   B There are too few desks to work at.
   C The catalogue is difficult to use.

Multiple-choice with single answer

Task guide

▶ This task requires you to choose the correct answer to each question from three possible answers.

▶ There may be between one and ten questions.

▶ The questions follow the order of the recording.

▶ Within each question, you may hear reference to the three options in any order.

▶ If you realise you have missed a question, don't try to remember it, but move on, and make sure you do not miss the next question(s).

▶ Multiple-choice questions vary considerably in terms of complexity. In Section 1, they ask you to listen for relatively straightforward facts, but in Section 3 and Section 4, the questions will test your understanding of opinions, feelings, evidence, argument, and so on.

▶ Do not immediately choose an option simply because you hear the same word or words on the recording. It is your understanding of the meaning of the whole question that is tested here.

▶ See also pages 7 and 10 for other types of multiple-choice tasks.

Step-by-step guide

▶ **Step 1 – Think first**

It is very important that you read the question carefully.

The stems of some questions (here *Questions 21 and 22*) are partial sentences, to be completed by the possible answers, while the stems of others are complete questions (here *Questions 23, 24 and 25*.)

▶ **Step 2 – Watch out for possible dangers**

Look at *Question 21*. The question consists of two parts: 'Before giving her presentation' and 'Kate was worried about'. This is what you must listen for.

These are some dangers in choosing an answer:

You hear Kate say what worried her during or after the presentation, not **before** her presentation, and choose the wrong answer.

You hear Kate say what she was looking forward to, not what she was **worried about** before the presentation, and choose the wrong answer.

You hear another speaker, not **Kate**, say what he or she was worried about before his or her presentation, and choose the wrong answer.

▶ **Step 3 – Consider the possibilities**

Look at the audio script for *Question 21* and answer the questions below about options A, B and C.

Audio script

I was ever so nervous beforehand. It's silly, because I do know my stuff quite well. I must know those statistics inside out, but when you have to get each table of results to come up in the right order, it can make you nervous. It was my first time using the computerised projector, and I was sure I was going to get the controls wrong, or something. And of course, that's not a good situation, if you know you've got to listen to questions carefully and be ready to answer quickly.

Option A

1 Did Kate expect to be asked questions? ....
2 Does she talk about questions being difficult? ....
3 Is option A the correct answer? ....

Option B

1 Does she talk about using projection equipment? ....
2 Does she talk about problems in connection with projection equipment? ....
3 Is option B the correct answer? ....

Option C

1 Does she talk about statistical results? ....
2 Does she say that explaining statistical results was something she was worried about? ....
3 Is option C the correct answer? ....

▶ **Step 4 – Listen and do the task**

Questions 26–30

Who will do the following tasks?

A   Martin
B   Kate
C   both Martin and Kate

Write the correct letter, **A, B** *or* **C** *next to questions 26–30.*

26   compose questionnaire   ....

27   select people to interview   ....

28   conduct interviews   ....

29   analyse statistics   ....

30   prepare visuals for presentation   ....

Classification

Task guide

▸ This task requires you to answer a series of questions with the same choice of answers in each case.

▸ Although the possible answers are the same for each question, the questions do not depend on each other. You can get one question wrong, but the next one right.

▸ Do not try to 'break the code': it is not possible to predict how many answers will be the same, or to find a pattern of any kind.

▸ In some cases, option C may be the combination of options A and B. In other cases, the possible answers may consist of three distinct possibilities – three different people, places, periods of time, and so on.

▸ The questions follow the order of the recording.

▸ If you miss one question, leave it and go on to the next one.

Step-by-step guide

▸ **Step 1 – Think first**

What you hear on the recording may be different words from the questions, but with the same meaning.

For 'compose a questionnaire' in *Question 26*, you might hear 'write a questionnaire', 'create a questionnaire', 'produce questions for a questionnaire', 'put a questionnaire together', and so on.

Look at *Questions 27–30*. Think of what you might hear on the recording and write your ideas:

27 ....

28 ....

29 ....

30 ....

▸ **Step 2 – Check what you will hear**

Look at the audio script for *Question 26*.

Audio script

Kate: Yes. Well, we're going to need the questionnaire before we can do much else, aren't we? Do you want to handle that?
Martin: I'd assumed we'd do it together?
Kate: You have more experience than me. Maybe you could think up the main questions, you know, a first version of the whole thing, and then I could read it through.
Martin: And make suggestions? Well, OK.

Kate first suggests that Martin 'handles' the questionnaire. If you choose option A (Martin) at this point, you are answering the question too soon. At this point, it has not been confirmed who will do the task of composing the questionnaire.

Next, Martin suggests that they do the task together. This indicates that both Martin and Kate (option C) is the answer. However, you cannot be sure, because Kate has not agreed to this yet.

Then Kate accepts Martin's suggestion and clarifies how they will both do the task. But you still cannot be sure, because Martin has not agreed to this.

Finally, Martin confirms his agreement ('Well, OK.'), and you can now safely choose option C as the correct answer.

▸ **Step 3 – Listen and do the task**

LISTENING MODULE	READING MODULE	WRITING MODULE	SPEAKING MODULE

SECTION 1
SECTION 2
SECTION 3
SECTION 4

▸ **Questions 31–40**

Questions 31–34

Answer the questions below.

Write **NO MORE THAN ONE WORD AND/OR A NUMBER** *for each answer.*

31 Where was a Stone Age rubbish dump found?

....

32 In Medieval times, what type of waste was most common?

....

33 What did science link with waste?

....

34 Which invention is the biggest problem for the environment?

....

Short-answer questions (1)

Task guide

▸ This task requires you to write answers to separate questions by using information you hear on the recording.

▸ The questions follow the order of the recording.

▸ Read the instructions carefully. Notice how many words you can use to answer each question. If you use more words than you are told, your answer will be wrong.

▸ You must write the exact words that you hear on the recording. Do not try to use other words or to change the form of words.

▸ Remember that the wording used in the questions is not likely to be exactly the same as the wording you hear on the recording. It is likely to be paraphrased or to use synonyms.

▸ Sometimes you may think you know the answer to a question from your general knowledge. But remember that these questions are about what the speaker says. You must answer the question according to what information the speaker gives on the recording.

▸ See also page 22 for another type of short-answer task.

Step-by-step guide

▶ **Step 1 – Think first**

Look at *Questions 31–34*, and think about the kinds of answers you are required to write.

Questions 31–34 are about facts. *Questions 31, 33* and *34* will need to be answered with nouns. *Question 32* will need to be answered with an adjective.

While multiple-choice questions often test your understanding of opinion rather than plain fact, in short-answer questions you need to listen for and extract facts.

▶ **Step 2 – Identify the correct answer**

This task is likely, particularly when used in Section 4, to involve dealing with more than one apparently possible answer. It's important to distinguish between what is apparently possible and what is correct.

Look at the audio script for *Questions 31* and *32* and answer the questions below.

Audio script

We have evidence that in ancient Greece and Rome governments operated municipal waste collection, and a huge Stone Age mound was identified some years ago in Norway as waste disposal, so we can see that people have been generating waste for a very long time indeed. However, during the Dark Ages, sophisticated municipal waste processing disappeared. The medieval answer to waste was to throw it out of the window. But this waste, apart from broken pottery and a few metal objects, was largely organic.

Question 31

1 This question asks 'where': which three places are mentioned in the audio script?

....

2 Which words in the audio script mean the same as 'rubbish dump'?

....

3 Which words in the audio script mean the same as 'was … found'?

....

4 What is the correct answer to *Question 31*?

....

Question 32

1 Can the words 'throw it out of the window' be an answer to *Question 32*?

....

2 Which three types of waste in medieval times are mentioned in the audio script?

....

3 What word in the audio script means the same as 'most common'?

....

4 What is the correct answer to *Question 32*?

....

▶ **Step 3 – Listen and do the task**

LISTENING MODULE   READING MODULE   WRITING MODULE   SPEAKING MODULE

SECTION 1
SECTION 2
SECTION 3
SECTION 4

Questions 35–37

List **THREE** *factors which led to the increase in waste.*

Write **NO MORE THAN TWO WORDS** *for each answer.*

35 ....

36 ....

37 ....

Short-answer questions (2)

Task guide

▸ This task requires you to answer the same question with a list of two or more things.

▸ The instructions tell you the maximum number of words you can use. Do not use more words than this.

▸ You can write your answers in any order.

▸ It is important that what you write in the list answers the question.

▸ See also page 20 for another type of short-answer task.

Step-by-step guide

▸ **Step 1 – Think first**

The question asks you to list 'factors which led to the increase in waste'.

Think of words which mean the same as 'factor'.
Think of words which mean the same as 'lead to'.
Think of words which mean the same as 'increase'.
Think of words which mean the same as 'waste'.

▸ **Step 2 – Select what to write**

Look at the audio script for *Question 35*. The correct answer is 'mass manufacturing'.

Audio script

As many countries became industrialised, we saw the advent of **mass manufacturing**. This has been enormously damaging as it has greatly increased the amount of things on the planet's surface which don't go away by themselves.

Why are these answers not correct?

1 industrialised

....

2 the advent of manufacturing

....

3 damaging

....

4 amount of things

....

▸ **Step 3 – Listen and do the task**

Questions 38–40

Which country uses the highest proportion of each method of waste disposal?

*Choose your answers from the box and write the letters **A–F** next to questions 38–40.*

> A Denmark
> B Germany
> C Japan
> D Switzerland
> E UK
> F USA

38 incineration: ....

39 landfill: ....

40 recycling: ....

Matching

Task guide

▸ This task requires you choose an answer for each question from the same list of possible answers.

▸ The options are usually listed alphabetically or similarly. For example, if the options are dates, they will be listed with the earliest first.

▸ The questions follow the order of the recording.

▸ You must read the question very carefully, as the possible answers will be mentioned several times in different ways.

Step-by-step guide

▸ **Step 1 – Read the question**

The question asks you to listen for the country 'which uses the highest proportion of each method of waste disposal'.

It is very likely that all the six countries listed will use all three waste disposal methods.

It is possible that a large country such as the US could incinerate 'a low proportion' of its waste, but this waste could be 'a higher quantity' of waste than that incinerated by another smaller country that incinerates 'a high proportion' of its waste.

Such questions will not depend on mathematics.

You need to read the question very carefully.

▸ **Step 2 – Check what you will hear**

Look at the audio script for *Question 38*.

Audio script

One of the main ways of dealing with MSW is incineration – burning it. This is adopted variously around the world. The UK burns relatively little waste, as does the US, while Denmark burns about half of all waste, and Japan uses this method for as much as three quarters.

You hear four countries, the UK, the US, Denmark and Japan, mentioned very closely together. The possible answers, A, C, E and F, are all heard, and you must be able to distinguish C as the only correct one.

▸ **Step 3 – Listen and do the task**

You should spend about 20 minutes on **Questions 1–13**, *which are based on Reading Passage 1 on pages 24 and 25.*

The Dollar-a-Year Man
How John Lomax set out to record American folk music

A In the early 1930s, folklorist, platform lecturer, college professor and former banker John Avery Lomax was trying to recapture a sense of direction for his life. For two decades he had enjoyed a national reputation for his pioneering work in collecting and studying American folk songs; no less a figure than President Theodore Roosevelt had admired his work, and had written a letter of support for him as he sought grants for his research. He had always dreamed of finding a way of making a living by doing the thing he loved best, collecting folk songs, but he was now beginning to wonder if he would ever realise that dream.

B Lomax wanted to embark on a nationwide collecting project, resulting in as many as four volumes, and 'complete the rehabilitation of the American folk-song'. Eventually this was modified to where he envisioned a single book tentatively called *American Ballads and Folk Songs,* designed to survey the whole field. It called for first-hand field collecting, and would especially focus on the neglected area of black folk music.

C In 1932, Lomax travelled to New York, and stopped in to see a man named H.S. Latham of the Macmillan Company. He informally outlined his plan to Latham, and read him the text of an earthy African American blues ballad called 'Ida Red'. Latham was impressed, and two days later Lomax had a contract, a small check to bind it, and an agreement to deliver the manuscript about one year later. The spring of 1932 began to look more green, lush and full of promise.

D Lomax immediately set to work. He travelled to libraries at Harvard, the Library of Congress, Brown University and elsewhere in order to explore unpublished song collections and to canvas the folk song books published over the past ten years. During his stay in Washington, D.C., Lomax became friendly with Carl Engel, Music Division chief of the Library of Congress. Engel felt that Lomax had the necessary background and energy to someday direct the Archive of Folk Song. Through funds provided by the Council of Learned Societies and the Library of Congress, Lomax ordered a state-of-the-art portable recording machine. More importantly, the Library of Congress agreed to furnish blank records and to lend their name to his collecting; Lomax simply had to agree to deposit the completed records at the Library of Congress. He did so without hesitation. On July 15, 1933, Lomax was appointed an 'honorary consultant' for a dollar a year.

E Together with his eighteen-year-old son Alan, he began a great adventure to collect songs for *American Ballads and Folk Songs*, a task that was to last for many months. Lomax's library research had reinforced his belief that a dearth of black folk song material existed in printed collections. This fact, along with his early appreciation of African American folk culture, led Lomax to decide that black folk music from rural areas should be the primary focus. This bold determination resulted in the first major trip in the United States to capture black folk music in the field. In order to fulfill their quest, the two men concentrated on sections of the South with a high percentage of blacks. They also pinpointed laboring camps, particularly lumber camps, which employed blacks almost exclusively. But as they went along, prisons and penitentiaries also emerged as a focal point for research.

F The recordings made by the Lomaxes had historical significance. The whole idea of using a phonograph to preserve authentic folk music was still fairly new. Most of John Lomax's peers were involved in collecting songs the classic way: taking both words and melody down by hand, asking the singer to perform the song over and over until the collector had 'caught' it on paper. John Lomax sensed at once the limitations of this kind of method, especially when getting songs from African-American singers, whose quarter tones, blue notes and complex timing often frustrated white musicians trying to transcribe them with European notation systems.

G The whole concept of field recordings was, in 1933 and still is today, radically different from the popular notion of recording. Field recordings are not intended as commercial products, but as attempts at cultural preservation. There is no profit motive, nor any desire to make the singer a 'star'. As have hundreds of folk song collectors after him, John Lomax had to persuade his singers to perform, to explain to them why their songs were important, and to convince the various authorities – the wardens, the trusties, the bureaucrats – that this was serious, worthwhile work. He faced the moral problem of how to safeguard the records and the rights of the singers – a problem he solved in this instance by donating the discs to the Library of Congress. He had to overcome the technical problems involved in recording outside a studio; one always hoped for quiet, with no doors slamming or alarms going off, but it was always a risk. His new state-of-the-art recording machine sported a new microphone designed by NBC, but there were no wind baffles to help reduce the noise when recording outside. Lomax learned how to balance sound, where to place microphones, how to work echoes and walls, and soon was a skilled recordist.

IELTS
TEST 1

Exam Essentials

| LISTENING MODULE | READING MODULE | WRITING MODULE | SPEAKING MODULE |

PASSAGE 1
PASSAGE 2
PASSAGE 3

Questions 1–5

Complete the summary below.

Choose **NO MORE THAN THREE WORDS** *from the passage for each answer.*

Write your answers in boxes 1–5 on your answer sheet.

JOHN LOMAX'S
P R O J E C T

Lomax began the research for this project by looking at **1** .... that were not available in book form, as well as at certain books. While he was doing this research, he met someone who ran a department at the **2** .... in Washington. As a result of this contact, he was provided with the very latest kind of **3** .... for his project.

Lomax believed that the places he should concentrate on were **4** .... in the South of the US. While he and his son were on their trip, they added **5** .... as places where they could find what they were looking for.

Summary (notes/table/flow chart) completion

Task guide

▸ This task requires you to find pieces of information in the reading passage in order to fill in the gaps in a summary (or notes or table or flow chart).

▸ This task often, but not always, focusses on one part or section of the reading passage, rather than on pieces of information spread throughout the text.

▸ This task requires you to use **exact words and phrases** from the text; the answers therefore all appear in the relevant part of the text. Do not try to use different words that have the same meaning – your answer will be marked wrong even if the meaning is correct.

▸ In completion tasks, the questions follow the same order as the relevant information in the reading passage.

▸ Read the instructions carefully. Notice how many words you can use to answer each question. The number of words may vary; you may be asked to write one, two or three words in each question. The instructions will also tell you if you need to use a number for your answer.

▸ In this case, you are asked to complete a summary. There is a flow-chart completion task on page 98, a table completion task on page 118 and a notes completion task on page 138. In all these tasks, the requirements are the same.

▸ See also page 80 for another type of summary completion task.

Step-by-step guide

▶ **Step 1 – Locate the task in the text**

First of all, you need to locate the task in the reading passage. Look for clues.

If the task has a title, it may refer to something that only appears in a particular section of the text.

In this case, the title ('JOHN LOMAX'S PROJECT') doesn't really help, because most of the text is about Lomax's project. You will need to look for clues in the summary.

1 The summary begins: 'Lomax began his research for this project ...'. In which section of the text (A–G) does he begin his research?

....

Which sentence in that section refers to him beginning his work?

....

2 The second sentence of the summary refers to Washington. Is Washington mentioned in the same section of the text?

....

3 The second paragraph of the summary mentions 'the South of the US'. Which section (A–G) of the text mentions 'the South'?

....

4 The second paragraph of the summary also mentions Lomax's son. Is his son mentioned in the same section of the text?

....

▶ **Step 2 – Find the answers**

Now look for the answers in the parts of the text you identified in step 1.

Remember that you must fill in the gaps with the exact words and phrases that appear in the text. However, the rest of the summary does not consist of words and phrases that are all repeated exactly from the text. Instead, the summary uses words and phrases that have the same meaning as those used in the text or that express the same ideas in a different way.

Question 1

Look at the words before and after the gap.

1 The verb after the gap is 'were'. What kind of word or phrase is required in the gap?

  A singular noun   **B** adjective   **C** plural noun

2 Which word in the text means 'look at' or 'study'?

....

3 Which word in the text means 'not available in book form?

....

Now use your answers for step 2 to find the answer to *Question 1*.

Question 2

Look at the sentence containing *Question 2*.

1 What is the word or phrase in the gap likely to refer to?
  A the name of a department
  B the name of an institution
  C the name of a person

2 Which word in the text means 'department'?

....

3 If someone 'runs' a place, they are the manager of it or in charge of it. Which word in the text means 'manager' or 'head'?

....

Now use your answers for step 2 to find the answer to *Question 2*.

Questions 3–5

Now answer *Questions 3–5* using the same process:

• Try to predict what kind of word is required in each gap by looking at the surrounding context.

• Look for words and phrases in the text that mean the same or express the same ideas as those used in the text surrounding the gaps in the summary.

IELTS TEST 1

Exam Essentials

LISTENING MODULE   **READING MODULE**   WRITING MODULE   SPEAKING MODULE

PASSAGE 1
PASSAGE 2
PASSAGE 3

Questions 6–10

Reading Passage 1 has seven sections labelled **A–G**.

Which section contains the following information?

Write the correct letter **A–G** *in boxes 6–10 on your answer sheet.*

NB *You may use any letter more than once.*

6   a reference to the speed with which Lomax responded to a demand

7   a reason why Lomax doubted the effectiveness of a certain approach

8   reasons why Lomax was considered suitable for a particular official post

9   a reference to a change of plan on Lomax's part

10   a reference to one of Lomax's theories being confirmed

Matching information to sections of text

Task guide

▸ This task requires you to find the sections in which specific pieces of information appear in the reading passage.

▸ It is possible that the same section will be the answer to more than one question. If this is the case, the instructions will tell you that you can use any letter more than once. However, it is also possible that a section or sections of the text will not be the answer to any of the questions. The instructions will not tell you if this is the case, but do not worry if you have not chosen a particular section as the answer to any of the questions, because this may be correct.

▸ Be careful not to choose a section as your answer simply because it contains something on the same general subject as the question. It is likely that more than one section will contain information connected with the question, but only one section will contain the precise piece of information asked for in the question.

▸ Beware of 'word spotting'. Do not choose a section as your answer simply because it contains a word that also appears in the question. Other sections may also contain that word. It is very unlikely that the correct answer will involve simply finding the same word in both the question and a certain section of the reading passage.

▸ See also pages 34 and 74 for other types of matching tasks.

Step-by-step guide

The best approach to this task is to:

- read the first question and then look through the text to find the answer to it.
- move to the next question and repeat the process.

Question 6

▶ **Step 1 – Decide what you are looking for**

1 The question refers to a 'demand' that Lomax responded to. Therefore, you are looking for:
   A something he was required to do
   B something he asked for
   C something he was given

2 *Question 6* refers to 'speed'. Therefore, you are looking for a reference to him doing something:
   A well or badly
   B quickly or slowly
   C easily or with difficulty

▶ **Step 2 – Find the answer**

Now use your answers for step 1 to find the answer to *Question 6*.

When you are looking through the text, look for something that matches the ideas or information contained in the question.

In many questions, you will not find words and phrases in the reading passage that mean exactly the same as those used in the question. Instead, you will need to find places in the passage which refer to the idea expressed in the question.

When you have located the section which contains the relevant piece of information, you will be able to answer these questions:

1 What was Lomax required to do?

....

2 Which phrase in the text means 'very quickly' or 'immediately'?

....

Now write your answer for *Question 6*.

Question 7

▶ **Step 1 – Decide what you are looking for**

1 The question refers to why Lomax 'doubted the effectiveness' of an approach. Therefore, you are looking for a reference to him:
   A finding out how something worked
   B explaining how something worked
   C thinking that something didn't work very well

2 The question refers to an 'approach'. In this context, you are likely to be looking for:
   A a route taken on a journey
   B a research method
   C a type of music

▶ **Step 2 – Find the answer**

Now use your answers for step 1 to find the answer to *Question 7*.

Look for references in the reading passage that match the ideas and information contained in the question.

When you have located the section which contains the relevant piece of information, you will be able to answer these questions:

1 Which approach did Lomax consider ineffective?

....

2 Which word in the text means 'disadvantages' and refers to this approach, in his opinion?

....

Now write your answer for *Question 7*.

Questions 8–10

Now answer *Questions 8–10* using the same process:

- Read each question carefully and make sure that you understand exactly what you are looking for in the text.
- Find the section of the reading passage which matches exactly the ideas and information contained in the question.

IELTS TEST 1

Exam Essentials

LISTENING MODULE   **READING MODULE**   WRITING MODULE   SPEAKING MODULE

PASSAGE 1
PASSAGE 2
PASSAGE 3

Questions 11–13

Choose **THREE** *letters* **A–F**.

Write your answers in boxes 11–13 on your answer sheet.

Which **THREE** *of the following difficulties for Lomax are mentioned by the writer of the text?*

A   finding a publisher for his research

B   deciding exactly what kind of music to collect

C   the scepticism of others concerning his methods

D   the reluctance of people to participate in his project

E   making sure that participants in his project were not exploited

F   factors resulting from his choice of locations for recording

Multiple-choice with multiple answers

Task guide

▶ This task requires you to select a specified number of options which correctly answer the question.

▶ This task requires you to ask yourself two things for each option: (a) Is it true according to the text? and (b) Does it correctly answer the question?

▶ Be careful! An option may be true, but it may not answer the question. For example, if you are asked to select 'problems', an option may refer to something that did happen in the text but was not actually a problem.

▶ In these tasks, the options follow the same order as the relevant information in the text.

▶ Sometimes there is one mark for each correct option you choose; sometimes there is only one mark for the whole task, and you have to choose all the correct options in order to get a mark. If only one question number is given, you will know that only one mark will be given. In this task, there are three question numbers (*Question 11, 12* and *13*), which means that three marks will be given.

▶ See also page 68 for another type of multiple-choice task.

Step-by-step guide

▸ **Step-by-step guide**

The best approach to this task is to:
- take each option one by one
- find the relevant place in the text and
- decide whether the option is one of the answers to the question or not.

Option A

▸ **Step 1 – Locate the option in the text**

Look at option A and then read through the text. Which section mentions a publisher?

....

▸ **Step 2 – Decide whether the option answers the question**

Look through the section you identified in step 1. Answer the questions below and decide whether option A is one of the answers or not.

1 What was the name of the publishing company Lomax visited?

....

2 What was the name of the man he went to see about publishing the book?

....

3 How long after they met did this man contact Lomax?

....

4 Did this man agree to publish Lomax's book?

....

Using your answers to these questions, decide whether option A refers to something that Lomax found difficult.

Option B

▸ **Step 1 – Locate the option in the text**

Look at option B and then read through the text. Which section contains three specific references to the kind of music Lomax decided to collect?

....

▸ **Step 2 – Decide whether the option answers the question**

Look through the section you identified in step 1. Answer the questions below and decide whether option B is one of the answers or not.

1 What kind of music did Lomax decide to collect?

....

2 What two reasons are given for Lomax deciding to collect this kind of music?

....

3 Is there a reference to any other kind of music he considered collecting?

....

4 Is there a reference to Lomax taking a long time to decide what kind of music to collect?

....

Using your answers to these questions, decide whether option B refers to something that Lomax found difficult.

Options C–F

Now look at options C–F and use the same process to decide whether each one is an answer or not:
- Find the relevant part of the text.
- Read that part of the text carefully to find out whether each of the options was something that caused Lomax a problem or not.

IELTS TEST 1

Exam Essentials

LISTENING MODULE **READING MODULE** WRITING MODULE SPEAKING MODULE

PASSAGE 1
PASSAGE 2
PASSAGE 3

▸ **Questions 14–26**

You should spend about 20 minutes on **Questions 14–26**, *which are based on Reading Passage 2 on pages 33–34.*

Questions 14–20

Reading Passage 2 has seven paragraphs **A–G**.

Choose the correct heading for each paragraph from the list of headings below.

Write the correct numbers **i–x** *in boxes 14–20 on your answer sheet.*

List of Headings

i	A less systematic style of teaching a class
ii	The commonest characteristics found in teachers
iii	A forceful method rarely recommended in teacher training
iv	The impact of teachers with a radical vision
v	A series of stages for classifying teachers
vi	A false assumption about effective teachers
vii	The attitude of many teachers towards pupils
viii	A way of bringing about change in individuals
ix	Getting results through careful consideration of pupils' needs
x	The importance of having a suitable personality

---

14 Paragraph **A**

15 Paragraph **B**

16 Paragraph **C**

17 Paragraph **D**

18 Paragraph **E**

19 Paragraph **F**

20 Paragraph **G**

A good teacher?

A As a teacher for the past 20 years, I have seen many good ones, and some, it's true, fit the stereotype: graduates with good degrees from so-called 'good' universities. A cardinal mistake is to think qualifications make a good teacher. When you're faced with 30 truculent children after lunch on a Friday afternoon, they don't count for much. Take Lesley, a high-powered business executive who I mentored as she trained to be a teacher. She had everything: a great degree, excellent organisational skills and good communication skills. Yet she crumbled in the classroom because she was so impatient with her pupils: nothing they did was good enough. Whereas her employees had tolerated her endless nit-picking, her pupils became demotivated and disaffected.

B David had a first-class degree. As his mentor, I observed him teach what I felt was a relatively well-behaved class of 12-year-olds. A quarter of an hour in, it was clear that none of the children had the slightest idea what he was talking about; the class began talking, then chucking his elaborate worksheets around the class. Ironically, it was his support teacher, who didn't have a degree at all, who rescued the lesson by explaining in clear English what was required. If you don't have the right personality, you'll suffer in the bear pit of today's classrooms. In my experience, there are four types of teacher who are effective: the despot, the carer, the charmer, and the rebel.

C I've come across many despotic teachers in my career. Everyone turns to them when the going gets really tough. They are nearly always very experienced teachers who know not only all the pupils but their parents too, having taught many of them. During my first year of teaching, one of my classes rioted, pushed all the furniture out of my room, and swore at me. I called in the despot of my school, the deputy head, and he blasted them away with a sound telling off. Most manuals don't advocate this approach to teaching, but I have to admit it can be very effective, even if morally dubious. Despotic teachers often extract fantastic work from their pupils, and rarely have to use their full armoury – their reputations are usually enough. They are often highly organised, making their classrooms into small fortresses, and in my experience nearly always achieve above-average results, because they teach the syllabus to the last letter.

D The opposite of the despot is the caring teacher. They become surrogate parents for their pupils. Many don't have degrees, and have been appointed as "mentors" or "support teachers" to help struggling pupils plan out their lives – working out ways in which they can do their work most effectively. Usually, pupils love seeing their mentors, and learn from them the vital skill of "taking responsibility for their own learning" (as it's known in the jargon). I've taught some pupils who were really going off the rails – skipping school, getting into fights – yet when they were taken under the wing of one of these teachers, they transformed and blossomed. Unlike the despot, the caring teacher works with lots of people: parents, other teachers, social workers. What she or he manages to do is make pupils see they can control and shape their own lives. The teacher might mother her charges to death in the process, but the end result is nearly always a happy pupil who has achieved very much against the odds.

E The charmer, on the other hand, is quite different from both these previous staples of the teaching profession. They can be a disorganised species, living off adrenaline and wits. They are frequently highly academic, and are in teaching to be mates with their pupils, to understand them and play with them. With this sort of teacher, the classroom becomes one great big, bouncing playground of learning. Take Martin, one of the best teachers I've come across, who would prepare his lessons on the hoof after reading the newspaper, and would totally change direction mid-lesson if hit by some new inspiration. He was very disorganised, but did everything with a wink and a smile.

IELTS TEST 1

Exam Essentials

LISTENING MODULE   **READING MODULE**   WRITING MODULE   SPEAKING MODULE

PASSAGE 1
PASSAGE 2
PASSAGE 3

F Finally, there's the most controversial but often most effective kind of teacher: the rebel. These teachers see school as a place that should aim to transform society, and they believe that our children have been brainwashed by our capitalistic society into making certain assumptions about inequality, exploitation, injustice. They see the classroom as the place where these children can be "deprogrammed" – and make amazing teachers because they are so passionate and persuasive. Even if you disagree with their politics, you have to admit they deliver blinding lessons, whatever their subject.

G But the crucial point here is that none of these teachers learned their skills by getting a good degree: they learned them on the job. All could improve by watching other good teachers in the classroom and learning from their techniques. However, there are some "generic" traits which should be borne in mind when discussing what's best for our schools. All the best teachers motivate their pupils to work hard, and assess them very regularly. There is now a great deal of research to suggest it is how you use your assessment of your pupils' achievements to plan and shape succeeding lessons, not your subject knowledge that is the determining factor of how well they achieve.

Matching headings to paragraphs

Task guide

▸ This task requires you to select the most suitable headings for the paragraphs of a reading passage.

▸ In the list of possible headings that you select from, some of the headings are not suitable for any of the paragraphs of the reading passage.

▸ This task requires you to decide what the main topic or point of each paragraph is. An option may refer to something that is mentioned in a certain paragraph of the text, but it may not be the correct answer because it is not the main point or topic of that paragraph.

▸ Beware of 'word spotting'. Do not choose a heading as your answer simply because it contains a word that also appears in a particular paragraph of the text. It is likely that the same word will also appear in other paragraphs.

▸ See also pages 28 and 74 for other types of matching tasks.

Step-by-step guide

The best approach to this task is to read each paragraph of the text one by one, and then look at the list of headings each time to select the appropriate one.

Question 14

▶ **Step 1 – Read the paragraph**

Read paragraph A carefully and identify the main topic.

▶ **Step 2 – Consider each option**

Look at each option and decide whether it matches the main topic of the paragraph. You will need to ask yourself the questions below in order to answer the question. Questions i–x refer to the corresponding options i–x.

i   Is the paragraph mainly about a style of teaching that is not done with thorough planning?

ii   Does the paragraph focus on the qualities most frequently seen in teachers?

iii   Does the paragraph mainly talk about the use of a method that is not generally encouraged in teacher training?

iv   Does the paragraph focus on the effects of teachers who have strong opinions about social issues?

v   Is the paragraph mainly about a process for putting teachers into different categories?

vi   Does the paragraph focus on an incorrect belief about effective teaching?

vii   Does the paragraph mainly consider an attitude that is commonly held by teachers towards pupils?

viii   Is the paragraph mainly about what can cause changes to happen in some people?

ix   Is the paragraph mainly about how to get the right results by thinking carefully about what pupils need?

x   Does the paragraph focus on how important personality is?

▶ **Step 3 – Choose the correct option**

When you have chosen your answer for paragraph A, check that it is correct by answering this question:

Which word in the heading you have chosen is similar in meaning to 'a false assumption' in paragraph A?

....

Question 15

▶ **Step 1 – Read the paragraph**

Repeat step 1 above for paragraph B.

▶ **Step 2 – Consider each option**

Repeat step 2 above.

▶ **Step 3– Choose the correct option**

When you have chosen your answer for paragraph B, check that it is correct by answering this question:

Which word in paragraph B has a similar meaning to 'suitable'?

....

Questions 16–20

Now follow the same process to decide on your answers for *Questions 16–20* (Paragraphs C–G):

• Read each paragraph carefully.

• Use the questions in step 2 above to help you choose the correct heading.

LISTENING MODULE   **READING MODULE**   WRITING MODULE   SPEAKING MODULE

PASSAGE 1
PASSAGE 2
PASSAGE 3

Questions 21–26

Do the following statements agree with the views of the writer in Reading Passage 2?

In boxes 21–26 on your answer sheet write

YES   *if the statement agrees with the views of the writer.*

NO   *if the statement contradicts the views of the writer.*

NOT GIVEN   *if it is impossible to say what the writer thinks about this.*

21   More difficult behaviour is often seen in pupils towards the end of the school day.

22   An in-depth understanding of his or her subject is key to enhancing a teacher's success.

23   Getting involved with those who are close to pupils can achieve positive effects.

24   Teachers who make friends with their pupils are not generally successful.

25   Despite failing to conform, certain teachers have an undeniable ability with pupils.

26   Good teachers accept that a pupil's enthusiasm for learning comes from within.

Yes/No/Not Given

Task guide

▶ This task requires you to understand views expressed or claims made by the writer of the text.

▶ To answer each question, you will need to ask yourself three questions:
1 Is the same view expressed in the text?
2 Is the opposite view expressed in the text?
3 Is there no view on this particular matter in the text?

▶ For an answer to be 'No', the writer must directly state something that makes the statement in the question incorrect.

▶ Questions to which the answer is 'Not Given' involve the writer saying something related to the statement in the question, but not expressing a view or making a claim on the specific point mentioned in the question.

▶ This task requires you to look very closely at what the writer does say, with regard to each of the questions.

▶ The questions follow the order in which the relevant issues are discussed or points mentioned in the text.

Step-by-step guide

The best way to approach this task is to:

- look at each question one by one
- locate the relevant part of the text
- study the question and that part of the text carefully and
- then decide on your answer.

Question 21

▶ Step 1 – Locate the relevant section of the text

Which section or sections of the text describe pupils' behaviour during a particular part of the day?

....

▶ Step 2 – Study the question carefully

Focus on the place(s) in the text you identified in step 1. Look carefully at the question and decide exactly what it means.

1 Which adjective in the relevant part of the text describes 'difficult behaviour'?

2 The question is asking if the author says that

A pupils generally behave worse when teachers are unprepared.

B pupils generally behave worse if their teachers are unqualified.

C pupils generally behave worse at certain times.

▶ Step 3 – Find the answer

Using your answers in step 2, read the relevant part of the text carefully and answer these questions:

1 Does the writer say it is common for pupils to behave badly after lunch on Friday afternoons?

....

2 Does the writer say that pupils lose motivation when teachers are impatient?

....

3 Does the writer say that well qualified doesn't really help when you need to motivate children?

....

Now use your answers for steps 2 and 3 to decide on the answer to *Question 21*.

Question 22

▶ Step 1 – Locate the relevant section of the text

1 Which section(s) of the text refer(s) to academic qualifications for teachers?

....

2 Which two teachers are mentioned as having good academic qualifications in their subjects?

....

3 Which teacher is mentioned in this part of the text as being successful in explaining things to pupils?

....

▶ Step 2 – Study the question carefully

Focus on the place(s) in the text you identified in step 1. Look carefully at the question and decide exactly what it means.

1 Which words in the relevant part of the text describe someone doing something in an effective way?

....

2 The question is asking whether the writer states that

A Good qualifications are likely to result in good teachers.

B Unqualified teachers can work very effectively with qualified ones.

C Qualifications are not the only factor in whether a teacher is good or not. Unqualified teachers can work very effectively with qualified ones.

▶ Step 3 – Find the answer

Using your answers in step 2, read the relevant part of the text carefully and answer these questions:

1 Does the writer say that Lesley's skills helped her to be successful as a teacher?

....

2 Does the writer say that David's class responded well to his teaching?

....

3 Does the writer suggest that a teacher with fewer qualifications in the subject achieved good results with pupils?

....

Now use your answers for steps 1 and 2 to decide on the answer to *Question 22*.

Questions 23–26

Now answer *Questions 23–26*, using the same process:

- Locate the relevant part of the text.
- Study the question and the relevant part of the text carefully.
- Ask yourself the three questions listed in the **Task guide** on page 36.

IELTS
TEST 1

Exam Essentials

LISTENING MODULE   READING MODULE   WRITING MODULE   SPEAKING MODULE
                    PASSAGE 1
                    PASSAGE 2
                    PASSAGE 3

*You should spend about 20 minutes on **Questions 27–40**, which are based on Reading Passage 3 below.*

The birth of our modern minds

When did we begin to use symbols to communicate? Roger Highfield reports on a challenge to prevailing ideas

Anyone who doubts the importance of art need do no more than refer to the current account of human evolution, where the emergence of modern people is not so much marked by Stone Age technology as a creative explosion that rocked Europe 40,000 years ago. Our ancestors began to adorn their bodies with beads and pendants, even tattoos; they painted representations of animals, people and magical hybrids on cave walls in Lascaux, France and Altamira in Spain. They sculpted voluptuous stone figures, such as the Venus of Willendorf. This cultural Big Bang, which coincided with the period when modern humans reached Europe after they set out, via the Near East, from Africa, marked a decisive point in our story, when man took a critical step beyond the limitations of his hairy ancestors and began to use symbols. The modern mind was born.

Or was it? Britain's leading archaeologist questions the dogma that the modern human mind originated in Europe and, instead, argues that its birth was much more recent, around 10,000 years ago, and took place in the Middle East. Lord Renfrew, professor of archaeology at Cambridge University, is troubled by what he calls the 'sapient behaviour paradox': genetic findings, based on the diversity of modern humans, suggest that our big brains emerged 150,000 years ago, when *Homo sapiens* evolved from *Homo erectus*, and were fully developed about 60,000 years ago.

But this hardware, though necessary, was not sufficient for modern behaviour: software (culture) is also required to run a mind and for this to be honed took tens of millennia. There is something unsatisfactory about the genetic argument that rests on the 'potential' for change emerging, he argues. Ultimately, little happened – or at least not for another 30,000 years.

Although there is no doubt that genes shaped the hardware of the modern brain, genetics does not tell the whole story. 'It is doubtful whether molecular sequences will give us any clear insights,' said Lord Renfrew, adding that the current account of our origins has also become sidetracked by placing too much emphasis on one cultural event. Either side of the boundary between the Middle and Upper Palaeolithic, 40,000 years ago, people lived much the same way. To the casual observer, the archaeological record for *Homo sapiens* does not look much different from *Homo erectus*'s, or even our beetle browed European cousins, the Neanderthals. 'There are detailed changes in tools and so on but the only one that really strikes you is cave art.'

And this artistic revolution was patchy: the best examples are in Spain and France. In Britain, the oldest known cave art consists of 12,000-year-old engravings in Creswell Crags. Indeed, was there an artistic revolution 40,000 years ago at all? Two pieces of ochre engraved with geometrical patterns 70,000 years ago were recently found at Blombos Cave, 180 miles east of Cape Town, South Africa. This means people were able to think abstractly and behave as modern humans much earlier than previously thought. Lord Renfrew argues that art, like genetics, does not tell the whole story of our origins. For him, the real revolution occurred 10,000 years ago with the first permanent villages. That is when the effects of new software kicked in, allowing our ancestors to work together in a more settled way. That is when plants and animals were domesticated and agriculture born.

'First there were nests of skulls and unusual burial practices, cult centres and shrines. Then you have the first villages, the first towns, like Jericho in Jordan (around 8000 BC) and Catalhöyük in Turkey (est 6500 BC), then the spread of farming to Europe. Before long, you are accelerating towards the first cities in Mesopotamia, and then other civilisations in Mexico, China and beyond.'

Living in timber and mud brick houses led to a very different engagement between our ancestors and the material world. 'I don't think it was until settled village communities developed that you had the concept of property, or that "I own these things that have been handed down to me".' This in turn could have introduced the need for mathematics, to keep a tally of possessions, and written language to describe them. In the Near East, primitive counters date back to the early farming period and this could have marked the first stages of writing, said Lord Renfrew. 'We have not solved anything about the origins of modern humans until we understand what happened 10,000 years ago,' he said. He is excited by excavations now under way in Anatolia, a potential birthplace of the modern mind, in Catalhöyük, one of the earliest places where close-knit communities were born, and Göbekli Tepe, a shrine that predates village life. These spiritual sites may have seeded the first human settled communities by encouraging the domestication of plants and animals.

IELTS TEST 1

Exam Essentials

LISTENING MODULE   **READING MODULE**   WRITING MODULE   SPEAKING MODULE

PASSAGE 1
PASSAGE 2
PASSAGE 3

Questions 27–32

Answer the questions below using **NO MORE THAN THREE WORDS** *for each answer.*

Write your answers in boxes 27–32 on your answer sheet.

27   According to the current view, what does NOT indicate the first appearance of the modern human?

28   What type of evidence does Lord Renfrew question in general?

29   What, apart from art, were the developments in the creation of 40,000 years ago?

30   What kind of cave art in Britain is referred to?

31   What TWO things does Lord Renfrew believe to have been established 10,000 years ago?

32   What TWO things did the notion of personal possessions lead to?

Short-answer questions

Task guide

▸ This task requires you to write answers for questions, using pieces of information that are given in the reading passage.

▸ Read the instructions carefully. Notice how many words you can use to answer each question. The number of words may vary; you may be asked to write one, two or three words in each question. The instructions will also tell you if you need to use a number in one or more answers.

▸ All the questions can be answered using actual words and phrases that appear in the reading passage. You are not required to think of words that have the same meaning as words in the text, and if you do this, you may make unnecessary mistakes.

▸ The questions follow the same order as the relevant information in the text.

Step-by-step guide

The best way to approach this task is to:

- look at each question one by one
- locate the relevant part of the text and
- look for the information that relates to each question.

For some questions, you may find words and phrases in the text that mean the same as words and phrases in the question. For some questions, this will not be the case, and you will have to look for information that matches the content of the question but is expressed in a different way.

Question 27

▶ **Step 1 – Locate the question in the text**

1 Find a sentence in the text that mentions the current view concerning the development of the modern human being. Which sentence is it and in which paragraph is it?

....

2 Which word in that sentence means 'first appearance'?

....

3 Which word in that sentence means 'indicated'?

....

▶ **Step 2 – Find the answer**

The sentence in the text you identified in step 1 refers to something that does indicate the first appearance of the modern human being, and something that does not.

Find these two things and choose one of them as your answer for *Question 27*.

Question 28

▶ **Step 1 – Locate the question in the text**

1 If you 'question' something, you have doubts about it or think it may not be right. In which paragraphs are there references to Lord Renfrew having doubts about something?

....

2 Which word in the relevant part of the text means 'worried' or 'concerned'?

....

3 Which word in the relevant part of the text means 'not right' or 'not good enough'?

....

▶ **Step 2 – Find the answer**

1 In the paragraph you identified in questions 2 and 3 of step 1, Lord Renfrew is said to have doubts about certain evidence. Which word in that paragraph means 'evidence' or 'discoveries'?

....

2 In the same paragraph, Lord Renfrew is also said to consider a certain opinion not to be right. Which word means 'opinion' or 'view' in this context?

....

3 Find a word in the text that is connected with the two words you identified in questions 1 and 2 above and write it as your answer for *Question 28*.

....

Questions 29–32

Now answer *Questions 29–32*, using the same process:

- Locate the question in the text.
- Look for sentences and phrases that relate to the content of the question.
- Remember that all the answers can be actual words and phrases that you find in the text.

IELTS TEST 1

Exam Essentials

LISTENING MODULE	**READING MODULE**	WRITING MODULE	SPEAKING MODULE

PASSAGE 1
PASSAGE 2
PASSAGE 3

Questions 33–40

Classify the following statements as referring to the period

A 10,000 years ago
B 40,000 years ago
C 60,000 years ago
D 70,000 years ago

Write the correct letter **A–D** *in boxes 33–40 on your answer sheet.*

33 The brain was completely formed physically but was not capable of all the functions of the modern mind.

34 There was a major change in the attitude of humans to each other.

35 A huge amount of art in different forms began to appear.

36 Development of the human mind occurred at the same time as a migration.

37 Art from the period casts doubt on the conventional view of the development of the human mind.

38 The modern mind developed in a different location from the one normally assumed.

39 The only significant change in the development of man is shown in the art produced.

40 Further research into the period is essential for accurate conclusions to be drawn on human development.

Classification

Task guide

▶ This task requires you to match pieces of information with the categories they belong in according to the text.

▶ Make sure that there is something in the text connected with the option you choose that matches exactly the statement in the question. Often, more than one option will have a connection with the statement in the question, but only one option will match it exactly.

▶ The categories will be listed in a logical order, for example, chronologically or in alphabetical order. Therefore, they may not match the order in which they are mentioned in the text. Make sure you do not get confused and accidentally write the wrong letter for an answer.

Step-by-step guide

The best way to approach this task is to first identify the parts of the text in which the categories are mentioned. If you locate the categories in the beginning, you will only need to keep looking at those parts of the text, rather than constantly having to look through the whole text for each question.

▸ **Step 1 – Locate the categories in the text**

Look through the text and find where the time periods A–D are mentioned.

In which paragraphs and where in those paragraphs are they mentioned?

A 10,000 years ago

....

B 40,000 years ago

....

C 60,000 years ago

....

D 70,000 years ago

....

▸ **Step 2 – Find the answers**

For some questions, there may be words and phrases in the text which mean the same as words and phrases used in the question.

However, classification tasks involve more than simply matching words and phrases of similar meaning. For many questions, you will have to understand ideas that are presented in the text and match them to the ideas contained in the questions.

Question 33

1 Look at the parts of the text you identified in step 1 and find the place that relates to *Question 33*. You are looking for references to the brain being completely formed and to something it lacked. In which paragraph are these references?

....

When you have found the right part of the text, you will be able to answer these questions.

2 Which phrase in the text means 'completely formed'?

....

3 What is the modern mind said to require that it did not have at that time?

....

4 How long did it take for the mind to become capable of this?

....

Now identify which time period (A–D) this part of the text relates to. Write your answer for *Question 33*.

Question 34

1 Look at the parts of the text you identified in step 1 and find the place that relates to *Question 34*. You are looking for references to a big change and to relationships between humans. In which paragraph are these references?

....

When you have found the right part of the text, you will be able to answer these questions.

2 Which word in the text that means 'major change'?

....

3 The text refers to something having a big effect. Which phrase in the text means 'started to have a big effect'?

....

4 What did humans start to do that represented a major change?

....

Now identify which time period (A–D) this part of the text relates to. Write your answer for *Question 34*.

Questions 35–40

Now answer *Questions 35–40* using the same process:

- Read the question and look through the parts of the text you identified in step 1.
- Find information in the text that matches the content of the question.
- Identify which time period (A–D) this information relates to.

You should spend about 20 minutes on this task.

The charts below show the number of French adults whose parents spoke a French regional language to them when they were children and the number who speak a French regional language to their own children.

Summarise the information by selecting and reporting the main features, and make comparisons where relevant.

Write at least 150 words.

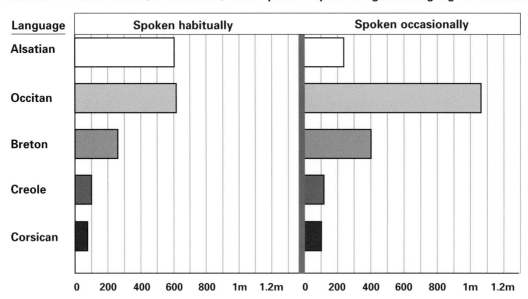

Number of French adults (in thousands) whose parents spoke a regional language to them in childhood

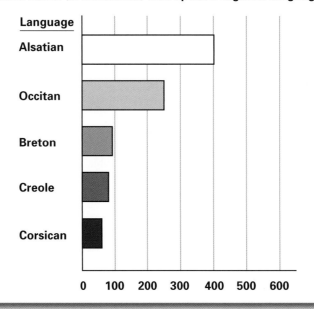

Number of French adults (in thousands) who speak a regional language to their own children

Describing charts and graphs

Task guide

▸ Tasks in the Writing Module will be marked according to the criteria described on page 84 – **content**, **organisation** and **use of language**.

▸ Many Task 1 questions involve statistical information in the form of bar charts, graphs or pie charts. Some tasks may involve a single chart or graph, others may involve more than one, and some may involve a combination of elements (for example, a graph and a bar chart).

▸ This task involves bar charts. You will find graphs, pie charts and combinations in the other tests in this book.

▸ You are required to **select the most important information and summarise it**. You should therefore begin by looking for the main points, the general trends or the overall message.

▸ **Do not list every fact and figure in your answer**. Include only the relevant main points, with relevant examples from the data. Do not include less important details.

▸ Do not become confused if there seems to be a lot of data. Even if there is more than one chart, graph, etc., there will usually be only one or two main points. Focus on finding these main points. Then decide which parts of the data best illustrate the main point or points.

▸ You are not required to do any mathematics for this task. Do not waste time adding and subtracting numbers. Concentrate on the general idea.

▸ If precise figures are not given in a chart or graph, do not waste time trying to decide what the precise figure is. Use words and phrases like: *approximately, about, roughly, (just) over, (just) under, nearly*, etc.

▸ Make sure that you write at least the minimum number of words specified in the instructions. Short answers will lose marks.

▸ On the other hand, do not write too much. If you write a very long answer, you may make mistakes and lose marks.

Step-by-step guide

▸ **Step 1 – Find the main point(s)**

1 Compare the third bar chart with the first two. What do you notice?
  A Some languages are spoken more by parents today than they used to be.
  B The numbers of people in the third chart are lower.
  C There has been little change for any of the languages.

2 A Which language was spoken to children the most in the past?

  ....

  B Approximately how many parents spoke this language to their children in the past?
     habitually ....
     occasionally ....
  C Approximately how many people now speak that language to their children?

  ....

3 A Which language is now spoken the most by adults to their children?

  ....

  B Approximately how many parents spoke that language to their children in the past?
     habitually ....
     occasionally ....
  C How many people now speak that language to their children?

  ....

4 Which language was spoken the least by parents to their children?

  ....

5 Is the number of parents speaking that language to their children now higher than the number whose parents spoke that language to them?

  ....

▸ **Step 2 – Organise your answer**

1 What should you begin your answer with?
  A a sentence about one of the languages

  B a sentence comparing two or more of the languages
  C a sentence comparing the tables in general

2 What should come next?
  A comparisons between the numbers who spoke each language habitually and the numbers who spoke each language occasionally
  B comparisons between each of the languages to indicate which were the most widely spoken in the past and which are the most widely spoken now
  C comparisons between how widely spoken languages were in the past and how widely spoken they are now

▸ **Step 3 – Language to use**

Write a sentence based on the information in the bar charts, using one word or phrase from each of these lists:

Linking phrases

although, even though, while, in the case of, as for, with regard to

....

....

Grammatical structures: comparison

a great deal lower than, not as many as, even greater than, far fewer than, not as high as

....

....

Vocabulary: increase and decrease

a rise in, a fall in, an increase in, a decrease in, rise, fall, go up, go down, drop, decline, be unchanged

....

....

Use your answers for steps 1, 2 and 3 to plan your answer.

Now write your answer for Task 1.

There is a sample answer on page 199.

You should spend about 40 minutes on this task.

Present a written argument or case to an educated reader with no specialist knowledge of the following topic.

> *In some societies, stress is now regarded as a major problem, and it is thought that people suffer from more stress than they did in the past.*
>
> *However, others feel that the amount of stress people have today is exaggerated. They say that previous generations were under more pressure, but the idea of suffering from stress did not exist.*
>
> *Discuss both these views and give your own opinion.*

You should use your own ideas, knowledge and experience and support your arguments with examples and relevant evidence.

Write at least 250 words.

Giving your opinion (1)

Task guide

▸ Tasks in the Writing Module will be marked according to the criteria described on page 86 – **content**, **organisation** and **use of language**.

▸ Task 2 requires you to give your opinion on an issue.

▸ The task consists of a statement or statements, followed by a question asking for your point of view.

▸ The instructions you are given are not always the same, and you must read them very carefully to make sure that you do exactly what you are asked to do.

▸ Some tasks focus on whether you agree or disagree with a statement. In tasks of this type, you may be asked the following questions:
(a) Discuss both these views and give your opinion.
(b) Do you agree or disagree?
(c) To what extent do you agree or disagree with this statement?
In this case, Task 2 is an example of (a). There are examples of (b) and (c) in other tests in this book.

▸ You must concentrate on presenting a clear and logical argument that the reader can follow easily.

▸ Divide your answer into paragraphs. Start a new paragraph for each new topic.

▸ Make sure that your answer is not too short (minimum 250 words), but also do not write a very long answer.

Step-by-step guide

▶ **Step 1 – Read the question carefully**

Look at Task 2. Which FIVE of the following should you do in your answer?

1 Give examples of types of people who suffer from stress today.

2 Discuss reasons why people suffer from stress today.

3 Suggest ways of dealing with stress.

4 Compare the amount of stress people have today with the amount of stress people had in the past.

5 Give examples of what life was like in the past.

6 Compare stress with other problems that people have today.

7 Give an opinion on whether too much attention is paid to stress today.

8 Give an opinion on whether stress will become a bigger problem.

▶ **Step 2 – Organise your answer**

Using your answers for step 1, make a plan for your answer:

• Make a note of which points you will include in your answer.

• Think of examples that can illustrate each point.

• Think about your conclusion.

Now write your notes:

Point 1: Stress today – types of people

....

Example(s)

....

Point 2: Stress today: reasons

....

Example(s)

....

Point 3: The situation in the past compared with today

....

Example(s)

....

Point 4: Life in the past: examples

....

Example(s)

....

Point 5: Opinion – attention paid to stress today

....

▶ **Step 3 – Language to use**

Using your notes for step 2, write a sentence using one word or phrase from each of these lists:

Linking words and phrases

• *in my opinion, in my view, The impression I have is..., It seems to me that...*

• *like, such as*

• *these days, nowadays*

....
....

Grammatical structures

• *used to do, be used to doing*

• *have to*

• *passive voice*

....
....

Vocabulary

• *under pressure, suffer from, stressful*

• *pace, hurry, rush, speed*

• *accept, complain, take for granted*

....
....

Now write your answer for Task 2.

There is a sample answer on page 199.

IELTS TEST 1

Exam Essentials

LISTENING MODULE   READING MODULE   WRITING MODULE   **SPEAKING MODULE**

PART 1
PART 2
PART 3

Part 1: Introduction and interview

Task guide

▸ In this part of the Speaking Module, the examiner will ask you a series of questions about yourself.

▸ You are expected to give more than 'yes' or 'no' answers. You are not expected to speak at great length in answer to any of the questions.

▸ There are no 'right' or 'wrong' answers; the examiner will ask you questions about things that you do, your likes and dislikes, and so on.

Step-by-step guide

▸ **Step 1 – Take the right approach**

The examiner's questions are designed to give you the opportunity to show that you can use your English to describe and explain things about yourself and familiar subjects, such as your country.

For example, the examiner may ask you about reading. You might be asked if you spend a lot of time reading. You are not being tested on how much reading you do, but on how well you explain how much reading you do (or don't do).

In this part of the test, try to behave as if you were having a normal conversation with people you know.

▸ **Step 2 – How much should I say?**

A good principle here is 'answer plus one'. Try to be generous, and offer a little extra information on the topic.

For example, if the examiner asks you how much time you spend reading, a basic answer is 'a lot' or 'not much'. Short answers, however, do not help a conversation develop very easily.

Look at these examples of 'answer plus one':

'A lot. I really enjoy reading, and I read every evening.'

'Not much. I don't have much free time, and I prefer to watch TV in the evenings.'

Part 1 – Example questions

Friends
a How much time do you spend with friends?
b What kinds of things do you like to do with your friends?
c What kinds of work or studies do your friends do?
d What does being a good friend mean to you?

▸ **Step 3 – Write your answers**

Look at the answers below. Then write your own answer to each question.

A How much time do you spend with friends?

Only a little. My studies take up most of my time.

....

....

B What kinds of things do you like to do with your friends?

It depends. In the winter, we go to the cinema. In the summer, it's nice just to sit in the park together, chatting.

....

....

C What kinds of work or studies do your friends do?

All sorts. Most of my friends are students like me, studying different subjects. One of my friends is a doctor, another one works for her father's business.

....

....

D What does being a good friend mean to you?

Oh, many things. I suppose the most important thing is trust. You must be able to trust each other.

....

....

IELTS
TEST 1

Exam Essentials

LISTENING MODULE   READING MODULE   WRITING MODULE   **SPEAKING MODULE**

PART 1
PART 2
PART 3

Part 2: Individual long turn

Task guide

▸ In this part of the Speaking Module, the examiner will ask you to give a short talk, or 'long turn', based on a task card that you will be given.

▸ The topic on the card will be a general and straightforward one.

▸ You are expected to speak continuously for between one and two minutes. The examiner will not ask you questions during your long turn.

▸ The examiner may ask you one or two short, easy questions when you have finished your long turn.

▸ The card you are given describes what you must talk about. It is important that you talk about this topic.

▸ The card includes three suggested points within the general topic. These are designed to help you decide what to say. If you do not talk about all of them, you will not lose marks.

Step-by-step guide

▸ Step 1 – Take the right approach

The long turn is designed to give you the opportunity to show how well you can speak in English on a subject that you are familiar with.

One or two minutes can seem like quite a long time, when you are the only person speaking.

Give yourself as much practice as you can for this task. You can practise speaking to yourself.

Because one or two minutes is quite a long time, you should use the opportunity to make notes before you start speaking. If you make a few notes, you will be able to structure your long turn.

▸ Step 2 – How should I organise what I say?

Making notes will help you organise what you say.

The notes you make may remind you of useful vocabulary and expressions to use, or of facts and points that you want to include in your long turn.

Part 2 – Example task

Read the topic card below carefully. You will have to talk about the topic for one to two minutes.
You have one minute to think about what you are going to say.
You can make notes to help you if you wish.

> **Describe a party you went to which you enjoyed.**
> **You should say:**
> ▸ **where the party was**
> ▸ **why the party happened**
> ▸ **who was at the party**
> **and explain why you enjoyed the party.**

▸ Step 3 – Make notes

Look at the notes and candidate's answer for each of the suggested points. Then write your own note and answer for the same points.

where the party was
Note: *parents' house*

....

Candidate: *I remember one party very well. It took place at my parents' house.*

....

why the party happened
Note: *brother's 21st*

....

Candidate: *The party was held to celebrate my brother David's twenty-first birthday.*

....

who was at the party
Note: *all family, D's friends*

....

Candidate: *Everybody in my family came. Some of them travelled from abroad to be there. And, of course, David had invited a lot of friends, too.*

....

why you enjoyed the party
Note: *seeing everybody, David adult*

....

Candidate: *I enjoyed this party because it made me feel wonderful to be surrounded by all my family, and also because it meant that my brother was now a real adult.*

....

IELTS TEST 1

Exam Essentials

LISTENING MODULE   READING MODULE   WRITING MODULE   **SPEAKING MODULE**

PART 1
PART 2
PART 3

Part 3: Two-way discussion

Task guide

▶ In this part of the Speaking Module, the examiner will ask you a series of questions related to the general topic of your 'long turn' in Part 2.

▶ These questions will be more demanding than the questions in Part 1. They will require you to give opinions, rather than simply explain facts.

▶ The questions will not test your general knowledge, but the way you express your ideas in English.

▶ It is important to give more than 'yes' or 'no' answers.

Step-by-step guide

▶ Step 1 – Take the right approach

The questions in this part of the test are designed to allow you to show that you can discuss things in English.

Part 1 and 2 focus on your own life and experiences. Part 3 encourages you to show you can express ideas that go beyond personal details.

The examiners assess your language abilities, not your opinions. Express your opinion freely and try to offer as much information on the topic as you can.

▶ Step 2 – What should I say?

In most of your answers to the examiner's questions, you will be expressing an opinion or giving some kind of interpretation.

You will not be stating simple facts.

You should try to introduce what you say with appropriate phrases for the kind of answer you give.

Part 3 – Example questions

A What kinds of social events are most popular in your country?

B What are the differences between the social events that older and younger people enjoy?

C Do you think it is a good idea for colleagues at work to spend time socially together?

D What changes have there been recently in social life in your country?

E Would you agree that technology can have negative effects on the way people spend their leisure time?

▶ Step 3 – Complete the answers

Match 1–5 with a–e to form complete answers.

1 I think it's difficult to judge. On the one hand, it gives us access to new kinds of entertainment

2 Well, I think it very much depends on people's different interests

3 It's become very different. Many people have a lot more money these days

4 I suppose that it is. It makes them enjoy their jobs more

5 I've noticed that older people prefer to spend their social time in each other's houses

a although of course they should also spend enough time with their families.

b and they like to spend it by going out in the evenings, much more than we used to.

c but, on the other, it means we spend a lot of time just sitting around, becoming unfit.

d while younger people want to go out to clubs, bars, and so on.

e but eating together is certainly very popular with everyone.

Now match the complete answers with the example questions A–E above.

Step-by-step guide

(continued)

▶ **Step 4 – Write your own answers**

Now write your own answers to questions A–E.
You can use expressions from the sample answers
in step 3.

A ....

....

B ....

....

C ....

....

D ....

....

E ....

....

LISTENING MODULE	READING MODULE	WRITING MODULE	SPEAKING MODULE

SECTION 1
SECTION 2
SECTION 3
SECTION 4

▶ **Questions 1–10**

Questions 1–10

Complete the form below.

Write **NO MORE THAN TWO WORDS AND/OR A NUMBER** *for each answer.*

COMPLAINT RECORD FORM

Holiday booked in name of:	**1** First name .... Last name ....
Address:	Flat 4
	2 ....
	Winchester SO2 4ER
Daytime telephone number:	**3** ....
Booking reference:	**4** ....
Special offer?	Yes, from **5** .... company
Insurance?	Yes, had **6** .... Policy
Type of holiday booked:	**7** .... Break
Date holiday commenced:	**8** ....
Details of complaint:	• no **9** .... at station
	• a **10** .... was missing

Form completion

Task guide

▶ This task requires you to complete a form by writing words and numbers that you hear on the recording.

▶ Read the instructions carefully. Notice how many words you can use to answer each question. The number of words may vary; you may be asked to write one, two or three words in each question. The instructions will also tell you if you need to use a number for your answer.

▶ Look at the form and think who might complete this form. When you listen to the recording, you will be able to follow which of the two speakers is actually completing the form.

▶ Do not change the words or numbers you hear. Write down exactly what you hear.

▶ The questions follow the order in which you hear the information on the recording.

▶ Form completion tasks in this section may ask you to write names of people or addresses that you have never heard before. These will usually be spelt out for you. Names, which are reasonably common English words, however, will not be spelt out for you.

Step-by-step guide

▶ Step 1 – Think first

Read through the form carefully. What sort of answer is required in each gap?

Remember that in the task here, you are told to write no more than two words and/or a number for each answer.

Decide if the gap will require:

A a word or two words

B a number

C a word or two words and a number

D a combination of numbers and letters

1 .... **2** .... **3** .... **4** .... **5** ....

6 .... **7** .... **8** .... **9** .... **10** ....

If you prepare yourself like this, you will find it easier to hear the answers on the recording.

▶ Step 2 – Check what you will hear

Look at this part of the audio script. The answers for *Questions 1–3* are in **bold**.

Audio script

Man: Oh no – let me just get a form ready … First, the name, please. Of the person who booked the holiday.
Woman: Well, our surname's **Sharpe. S–H** …
Man: Like a knife?
Woman: Yes, but with an E on the end.
Man: And a first name?
Woman: I'm Alice, but I think it was my husband who actually booked the trip – his name's **Andrew**.
Man: Fine. And then the address, please.
Woman: It's Flat 4, **Beaconsfield – that's B-E-A-C-O-N-S-F-I-E-L-D – House**. That's Winchester, and it's S-O-2, er, 4-E-R.
Man: Thank you. And could I take a telephone number?
Woman: We're on 0374 56561 at home, or – do you mean during the day? – then my work number's **0374 double-5 793**.
Man: I'll put the work one down, assuming that's normal office hours?
Woman: Oh yes.

It is important to make sure that you follow the requirements of the form as you listen.

For *Question 1*, the form asks for the 'first' name first, then the 'surname'. The woman, however, gives the surname first and the first name second.

Notice that because 'sharp' is a common word, you are expected to be able to spell it, and to add the 'E' at the end of the word. You are also expected to know the common first name, Andrew.

However, you are not expected to know 'Beaconsfield', and so this is spelt out for you. You are expected to know the word 'house'.

For the telephone number, it is again important to follow the requirements of the form. Have a look at *Question 3*. You are listening for a daytime telephone number. You should not simply write down any telephone number you hear.

▶ Step 3 – Listen and do the task

LISTENING MODULE	READING MODULE	WRITING MODULE	SPEAKING MODULE

SECTION 1
SECTION 2
SECTION 3
SECTION 4

▶ **Questions 11–20**

Questions 11–15

Complete the table below.

Choose your answers from the box and write the appropriate letters **A–H** *next to questions 11–15.*

> A driving licence
> B flexible working week
> C free meals
> D heavy lifting
> E late shifts
> F training certificate
> G travel allowance
> H website maintenance

TEMPORARY HOTEL JOBS

JOB	EMPLOYER	NOTES
Reception Assistant	Park Hotel	• 11 ...... • foreign languages • 12 ......
General Assistant	Avenue Hotel	• low pay • 13 ...... • 14 ......
Catering Assistant	Hotel 56	• free uniform • 15 ...... • outside city

Table completion (with choices)

Task guide

▶ This task requires you to complete a table by selecting from a list of possible answers.

▶ Some of the information in the table will already be filled in. You can use the location of this information to help you follow the information on the recording.

▶ You should read the list of possible answers carefully. Some of the options are likely to be similar, and you will need to make sure you choose correctly.

▶ Do not choose an option simply because it contains one or more words you may hear on the recording. Select your answer according to the meaning of what you hear.

▶ Write only the letter of the option you choose. Do not copy out the words of the option.

▶ Sometimes, a gap may have other words before and/or after it. If this is the case, make sure the answer you choose fits grammatically into the gap.

▶ Possible answers may also be provided for forms and other tasks.

▶ See also page 12 for another type of table completion task.

Step-by-step guide

▶ **Step 1 – Think first**

You don't have to write anything except letters in this task.

There are twice as many possible answers here as there are questions. Therefore, the challenge is to select from more than one likely option.

You can prepare for this by checking which options may be rather similar to each other. For example, options A and G refer to transport, and options B and E refer to the time of working.

▶ **Step 2 – Check what you will read and hear**

Reading the table carefully will help you follow the recording. You know that after 'Reception Assistant' and 'Park Hotel' are mentioned, you must be ready to answer *Question 11*. You also know that you must answer *Question 11* before you hear 'foreign languages' on the recording.

Look at the audio script for *Question 11*.

Audio script

The first job is Reception Assistant, and there are three vacancies for this position at the Park Hotel. This is quite a varied job, and in fact I should point out that at certain times of the day, it will involve heavy lifting when guests' luggage arrives, or perhaps deliveries come in, so bear that in mind when deciding whether to apply for this post.

Now look at options A–H. The job is described as 'varied', which might relate to 'flexible' in option B. 'Certain times of day' might be leading to 'late shifts' in option E. There is a clear reference to the job involving 'heavy lifting when guests' luggage arrives, or perhaps deliveries come in', which means that option D is the correct answer. Option D fully connects with what the speaker says, while options B and E only connect with part of what the speaker says.

▶ **Step 3 – Listen and do the task**

LISTENING MODULE	READING MODULE	WRITING MODULE	SPEAKING MODULE

SECTION 1
SECTION 2
SECTION 3
SECTION 4

Questions 16–20

Complete the flow chart below.

Write **NO MORE THAN TWO WORDS** *for each answer.*

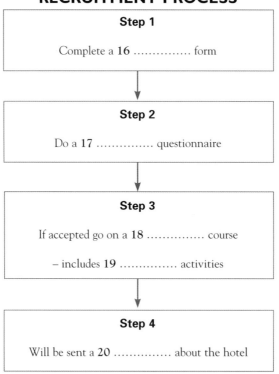

RECRUITMENT PROCESS

Step 1

Complete a **16** .... form

Step 2

Do a **17** .... questionnaire

Step 3

If accepted go on a **18** .... course

– includes **19** .... activities

Step 4

Will be sent a **20** .... about the hotel

Flow chart completion

Task guide

▸ This task requires you to complete a flow chart by writing answers that are pieces of information you hear on the recording.

▸ The flow chart is used to represent a process, so it is important that you follow the different stages or steps of the process described on the recording.

▸ Read the instructions carefully. Notice how many words you can use to answer each question.

▸ Make sure that the word(s) you write fit grammatically with the words around the gap.

▸ Write exactly the word(s) and/or numbers that you hear. Do not try to change them in any way – your answer will be wrong if you do.

▸ It is likely that you will hear more than one piece of information that could seem possible for each gap. Only one will in fact be correct, so listen very carefully.

Step-by-step guide

▸ **Step 1 – Think first**

The task asks you to write a word or two words in each gap. Make sure you are ready to write the word or words as soon as you hear the information on the recording.

Think about what you might hear in relation to the flow chart.

1 How might 'Step 1' or 'Step 2' be expressed?

2 How might 'complete' be said?

Remember, it is unlikely that the speaker will use exactly the same words in the same order as in the flow chart. However, your task is to write in the words you hear for the gaps.

▸ **Step 2 – Check what you will hear**

Look at this part of the audio script. The answers for *Questions 16* and *17* are in **bold**.

Audio script

So the first thing you'll need to do is fill in one of these, a **personal information** form. It's pretty straightforward and should only take you a few minutes. Once you've done that and handed it in, we'll give you a questionnaire about your **skills** to do. Again, I don't expect this to take you very long.

'The first thing you'll need to do' refers to 'Step 1' on the flow chart. 'Complete' is 'fill in'.

'Step 2' is expressed as 'once you've done that'.

'Personal information' comes immediately before 'form' in the audio script and in the flow chart.

'Skills', however, comes after 'questionnaire' in the audio script, but before 'questionnaire' in the flow chart.

▸ **Step 3 – Listen and do the task**

SECTION 1
SECTION 2
SECTION 3
SECTION 4

▶ **Questions 21–30**

Questions 21–26

Complete the sentences below.

Write **NO MORE THAN THREE WORDS** *for each answer.*

21 David feels that progress on the project has been slow because other members of the group are
    not …………………………………….. .

22 Jane thinks that ………………………………….. were not clearly established.

23 Dr Wilson suggests that the group use the …………………………….. available from the Resource Centre.

24 David doubts that the research will include an adequate ……………………………. .

25 According to Dr Wilson, the ……………………………. is now the most important thing to focus on.

26 Jane believes the group could make more use of some ……………………………. .

Sentence completion

Task guide

- ▶ This task requires you to complete sentences by writing in information you hear on the recording.

- ▶ Read the sentences carefully so that you are ready for the information when it occurs on the recording.

- ▶ The questions follow the order of the recording.

- ▶ The order of information within each sentence may be different from that on the recording.

- ▶ The words used in the sentences will usually be synonyms or paraphrases of the words that you hear on the recording – the words will be different, but the meaning will be the same.

- ▶ Read the instructions carefully. Notice how many words you can use to answer each question. If you use more words, your answer will be wrong.

- ▶ For each gap, write the exact words that you hear – do not change their form in any way.

- ▶ After you have filled in the gap, check that the sentence is grammatically correct and makes sense.

Step-by-step guide

▶ **Step 1 – Think first**

Firstly, make sure you are clear which speaker each sentence refers to.

Then, prepare for this task by thinking about how the wording of the sentences might be expressed on the recording.

▶ **Step 2 – Check what you will hear**

Look at the audio script for *Question 21*.

Audio script

David: Well, we anticipated problems of various kinds. None of the group has much experience of collaborating on projects. But we spent some time discussing how to go about it, and thrashed out what seemed a useful approach, but it seems that Jane and I are the only ones actually following the plan. That's meant that the whole project has been lacking coordination and so we've fallen behind our schedule.

1 What is the correct answer to *Question 21*?

....

2 What words and/or phrases might you write for *Question 21* if you didn't listen carefully?

....

3 How is 'progress on the project has been slow' represented in the audio script?

....

4 Why should you not write 'actually' as part of your answer to *Question 21*?

....

▶ **Step 3 – Listen and do the task**

Questions 27–30

Complete the timetable below.

Choose your answers from the box and write the letters **A–H** *next to questions 27–30.*

A	Compare photographs at newspaper offices.
B	Interview a local historian.
C	Listen to tapes in the City Library.
D	Study records of shop ownership.
E	Take photographs of the castle area.
F	Talk to the archivist at the City Library.
G	Tour city centre using copies of old maps.
H	Visit an exhibition at the University Library.

MON – WED: FIELD TRIP TO CAMBRIDGE

Mon 22nd	am	arrive at hotel
	pm	27 ....
Tues 23rd	am	28 ....
	pm	free time
Wed 24th	am	29 ....
	pm	30 ....

Timetable completion

Task guide

▸ This task requires you to complete a timetable by choosing from a list of possible answers.

▸ 'Timetable' can be any kind of timetable, diary, agenda, programme, etc.

▸ The speaker(s) on the recording will talk about the events in the timetable in the same order as the timetable you are given to complete.

▸ Write only the letter of the option you choose. Do not copy out the words of the option.

▸ Read and check the list of possible answers carefully. The possible answers are usually similar, and you need to choose between them.

▸ The possible answers are usually listed alphabetically.

▸ Sometimes, there may be some discussion among the speakers about exactly what will happen when. If this is the case, make sure that you choose the answer that is the one the speakers agree about, not just one that one of the speakers mentions.

▸ You may also encounter a timetable completion task in which you are not given a list of possible answers. In this case, you will have to write in the answers in words and/or numbers, as in table or notes completion tasks.

Step-by-step guide

▶ **Step 1 – Think first**

There are eight possible answers, but only four questions.

You need to read the possible answers very carefully, so that you are ready to choose between them quickly and correctly at the relevant points on the recording.

Try to be ready to distinguish between very similar possibilities. For example, there are three options with reference to libraries, but there's reference to two libraries in the audio script.

▶ **Step 2 – Check what you will hear**

Look at the audio script for *Question 27*.

Audio script

I've arranged for you to have a look at some useful visual material, especially photographs and old magazines and newspapers, which is included in an exhibition at the library in the university.

The word 'visual' might refer to option A ('photographs'), option E ('photographs'), option G ('old maps') and option H ('exhibition').

Which options might these words on the recording relate to?

1 photographs: ....

2 newspapers: ....

3 exhibition: ....

4 library: ....

5 university: ....

Which is the correct answer to *Question 27*?

▶ **Step 3 – Listen and do the task**

LISTENING MODULE	READING MODULE	WRITING MODULE	SPEAKING MODULE

SECTION 1
SECTION 2
SECTION 3
SECTION 4

▶ **Questions 31–40**

Questions 31–35

Complete the summary below.

Write **NO MORE THAN TWO WORDS** *for each answer.*

THE LONDON EYE

The architects who designed the London Eye originally drew it for a **31** .... in 1993.

Subsequently, they formed a partnership with **32** .... to develop the project. As the biggest

observation wheel ever built, its construction involved 1,700 people in five countries. Most of its components

had to be **33** .... , and delivering them had to be coordinated with the **34** ....

in the River Thames. On average, 350 hours a week are spent on maintenance of the Eye, and only

35 .... is used to clean the glass.

Summary completion

Task guide

▶ This task requires you to complete a summary by writing words you hear on the recording.

▶ You should read the summary through before the recording starts so that you have a general understanding.

▶ Read the instructions carefully. Notice how many words you can use to answer each question. If you use more words, your answer will be wrong.

▶ The questions follow the order of the recording.

▶ You can use the information provided in the summary to help you follow the recording.

▶ The words used in the given text of the summary will not be the same words as in the recording, but they will have the same meaning.

▶ When you complete the summary, don't change the form of the words you hear on the recording.

▶ When you read the summary through before listening, you may feel that you can answer some questions from your general knowledge. If this is the case, you must still listen very carefully to check if these are the correct answers on the recording.

Step-by-step guide

▸ **Step 1 – Think first**

To complete this task successfully:

• You must understand the meaning of the summary and the meaning of the recording.

• You must write the right number of correctly spelt words in the gaps.

• You must understand that the recording will contain more information than the summary, and be able to identify the relevant information on the recording.

▸ **Step 2 – Check what you will hear**

Look at the audio script for *Questions 31* and *32*.

Audio script

Its <u>creators</u> are husband and wife, <u>architects</u> David Marks and Julia Barfield. It was on their *kitchen table* in South London in 1993 that the <u>first drawings for the London Eye were made</u>, as the couple, who usually worked directly for *clients*, were entering **a competition**, the brief of which was to design *millennium landmarks* for the *capital*.

In fact, nobody won, and the whole idea was scrapped, but the couple remained convinced that their dream should be pursued. They started to piece the project together, and were soon attracting the attention of *the press*, and it wasn't long before **British Airways** had started to show an interest and then <u>became a partner</u>.

The words which lead you to the correct answers are <u>underlined</u>.

The correct answers are in **bold**.

Words which you might wrongly think could be the answers are in *italics*.

Notice that the words leading you to the correct answer may not be next to the actual answer on the recording.

After you have filled in a gap, check that the answer makes sense and is grammatically correct.

▸ **Step 3 – Listen and do the task**

Questions 36–40

Label the diagram below.

Write **NO MORE THAN TWO WORDS** *for each answer.*

rim

spindle

passenger capsule

39 mounting ....

38 ....

plinth

37 ....

40 ....

36 .... piles

Labelling a map/plan/diagram (3)

Task guide

▶ This task requires you to complete the labelling of a diagram by writing words you hear on the recording.

▶ If the words needed for the answers are very technical, they will be provided for you in a list of possible answers.

▶ Read the instructions carefully. Notice how many words you can use to answer each question. If you use more words, your answer will be wrong.

▶ You may need to write the whole of a label or part of a label.

▶ The questions follow the order of the recording.

▶ Write the exact word(s) that you hear on the recording. Do not change them in any way.

▶ See also pages 8 and 14 for other types of labelling tasks.

Step-by-step guide

▶ Step 1 – Put yourself in the picture

Look carefully at the diagram before you listen.

Try to form an independent understanding of what the diagram represents. Think about how this might be presented on the recording. For example, notice which parts are above or below other parts.

If the diagram shows an object that you are familiar with, you might think that you can answer some of the questions. However, remember that the task is to label the diagram according to what you hear on the recording, not according to your general knowledge.

▶ Step 2 – Check what you will hear

Look at the audio script for *Questions 36, 37* and *38*.

Audio script

The starting point was, of course, the ground, and while parts of the wheel itself were still being constructed in various countries, **tension** piles were being driven into the *ground* beside the River Thames. This was the first *step*, and once these were securely in place, a **base cap** was installed over them as a kind of *lock*, with two giant plinths pointing up, onto which an **A-frame** was attached, like a giant *letter*.

The correct answers are in **bold**. Words which you might wrongly think could be the answers are in *italics*.

Notice how the speaker guides you around the diagram, mentioning the 'starting point', the 'ground', explaining that the 'base cap was installed over them (tension piles)', and so on.

If you realise you have missed one question, focus carefully for the next one. It should be possible to find each answer independently of the other(s).

▶ Step 3 – Listen and do the task

IELTS
TEST 2

Exam Essentials

LISTENING MODULE   **READING MODULE**   WRITING MODULE   SPEAKING MODULE

PASSAGE 1
PASSAGE 2
PASSAGE 3

*You should spend about 20 minutes on **Questions 1–13**, which are based on Reading Passage 1 on pages 66 and 67.*

Emigration to the US

American history has been largely the story of migrations. That of the hundred years or so between the Battle of Waterloo and the outbreak of the First World War must certainly be reckoned the largest peaceful migration in recorded history; probably the largest of any kind, ever. It is reckoned that some thirty-five million persons entered the United States during that period, not to mention the large numbers who were also moving to Argentina and Australia. Historians may come to discern that in the twentieth and later centuries this movement was dwarfed when Africa, Asia and South America began to send out their peoples; but if so, they will be observing a pattern, of a whole continent in motion, that was first laid down in nineteenth-century Europe. Only the French seemed to be substantially immune to the virus. Otherwise, all caught it, and all travelled. English, Irish, Welsh, Scots, Germans, Scandinavians, Spaniards, Italians, Poles, Greeks, Jews, Portuguese, Dutch, Hungarians, Czechs, Croats, Slovenes, Serbs, Slovaks, Ukrainians, Lithuanians, Russians, Basques. There were general and particular causes.

As regards the general causes, the rise in population meant that more and more people were trying to earn their living on the same amount of land; inevitably, some were squeezed off it. The increasing cost of the huge armies and navies, with their need for up-to-date equipment, that every great European power maintained, implied heavier and heavier taxes which many found difficult or impossible to pay, and mass conscription, which quite as many naturally wanted to avoid. The opening up of new, superbly productive lands in the United States, Canada, Australia and New Zealand, coupled with the availability of steamers and steam trains to distribute their produce, meant that European peasants could not compete effectively in the world market: they would always be undersold, especially as the arrival of free trade was casting down the old mercantilist barriers everywhere. Steam was important in other ways too. It became a comparatively easy matter to cross land and sea, and to get news from distant parts. The invention of the electric telegraph also speeded up the diffusion of news, especially after a cable was successfully laid across the Atlantic in 1866. New printing and paper-making machines and a rapidly spreading literacy made large-circulation newspapers possible for the first time. In short, horizons widened, even for the stay-at-home. Most important of all, the dislocations in society brought about by the French Revolution, the Industrial Revolution and the various wars and tumults of nineteenth-century Europe shattered the old ways. New states came into being, old ones disappeared, frontiers were recast, the laws of land-tenure were radically altered, internal customs barriers and feudal dues both disappeared, payment in money replaced payment in kind, new industries stimulated new wants and destroyed the self-sufficiency of peasant households and the saleability of peasant products. The basic structure of rural Europe was transformed. Bad times pushed, good times pulled

(American factories were usually clamouring for workers): small wonder that the peoples moved.

Particular reasons were just as important as these general ones. For example: between 1845 and 1848 Ireland suffered the terrible potato famine. A million people died of starvation or disease, a million more emigrated (1846-51). Matters were not much better when the Great Famine was over: it was followed by lesser ones, and the basic weaknesses of the Irish economy made the outlook hopeless anyway. Mass emigration was a natural resort, at first to America, then, in the twentieth century, increasingly, to England and Scotland. Emigration was encouraged, in the Irish case as in many others, by letters sent home and by remittances of money. The first adventurers thus helped to pay the expenses of their successors. Political reasons could sometimes drive Europeans across the Atlantic too. In 1848 some thousands of Germans fled the failure of the liberal revolution of that year (but many thousands emigrated for purely economic reasons).

If such external stimuli faltered, American enterprise was more than willing to fill the gap. The high cost of labour had been a constant in American history since the first settlements; now, as the Industrial Revolution made itself felt, the need for workers was greater than ever. The supply of Americans was too small to meet the demand: while times were good on the family farm, as they were on the whole until the 1880s, or while there was new land to be taken up in the West, the drift out of agriculture (which was becoming a permanent feature of America, as of all industrialized, society) would not be large enough to fill the factories. So employers looked for the hands they needed in Europe, whether skilled, like Cornish miners, or unskilled, like Irish navvies. Then, the transcontinental railroads badly needed settlers on their Western land grants, as well as labourers: they could not make regular profits until the lands their tracks crossed were regularly producing crops that needed carrying to market. Soon every port in Europe knew the activities of American shipping lines and their agents, competing with each other to offer advantageous terms to possible emigrants. They stuck up posters, they advertised in the press, they patiently asnwered inquiries, and they shepherded their clients from their native villages, by train, to the dockside, and then made sure they were safely stowed in the steerage.

IELTS TEST 2

Exam Essentials

LISTENING MODULE	READING MODULE	WRITING MODULE	SPEAKING MODULE

PASSAGE 1
PASSAGE 2
PASSAGE 3

Question 1

Choose the correct letter **A**, **B**, **C** *or* **D**. *Write it in box 1 on your answer sheet.*

1   Which of the following does the writer state in the first paragraph?

    A   The extent of emigration in the nineteenth century is unlikely to be repeated.

    B   Doubts may be cast on how much emigration there really was in the nineteenth century.

    C   It is possible that emigration from Europe may be exceeded by emigration from outside Europe.

    D   Emigration can prove to be a better experience for some nationalities than for others.

Multiple-choice with single answer

Task guide

- This task normally consists of questions which each focus on a particular section of the text, rather than on information spread throughout the text.

- The exception to this is a 'global' question, which asks about the text as a whole (for example, the writer's purpose in the whole text). A global question is always the last question on a text.

- If there are several multiple-choice questions, these follow the order of the relevant information in the text.

- Multiple-choice questions often test your understanding of complex information or opinions, and require you to read the relevant section of the text very carefully.

- Make sure that the option you choose correctly answers the question you have been asked. Sometimes an option may be true according to the text, but not answer the actual question that has been asked.

- See also page 30 for another type of multiple-choice task.

Step-by-step guide

▸ **Step 1 – Locate the question in the text**

Read the question carefully and locate the relevant section of the text. In this case, you don't have to locate the section because the question tells you where to look ('first paragraph'). If it does not, it will normally refer to something that can easily be located in the text.

▸ **Step 2 – Find the answer**

Read the first paragraph carefully and answer the questions about options A–D.

Option A

1 Does the writer say that this particular migration may be the largest until now?

....

2 Does the writer say that such large-scale emigration will not happen again?

....

Option B

1 Does the writer say how many people are believed to have emigrated to the US in this period?

....

2 Does the writer question any statistics?

....

Option C

1 Does the writer make any predictions concerning emigration?

....

2 If something is 'dwarfed' by something else, is it bigger or smaller than that?

....

Option D

1 Does the writer compare any nationalities?

....

2 Does the writer refer to what happened to people when they had emigrated?

....

Now answer *Question 1.*

IELTS
TEST 2

Exam Essentials

LISTENING MODULE   **READING MODULE**   WRITING MODULE   SPEAKING MODULE

PASSAGE 1
PASSAGE 2
PASSAGE 3

Questions 2–9

Complete the sentences below with words taken from Reading Passage 1.

Use **NO MORE THAN THREE WORDS** *for each answer.*

Write your answers in boxes 2–9 on your answer sheet.

GENERAL CAUSES OF EMIGRATION TO THE US

- Population increases made it impossible for some to live from agriculture.

- In Europe, countries kept **2** .... that were both big, and this resulted in increases in **3** .... and in **4** .... , which a lot of people wanted to escape.

- It became impossible for **5** .... in Europe to earn a living because of developments in other countries and the introduction of **6** ....

- People knew more about the world beyond their own countries because there was greater **7** ....

- **8** .... had been formed because of major historical events.

- The creation of **9** .... caused changes in demand.

Sentence completion (1)

Task guide

- ▶ This task requires you to complete individual sentences with pieces of information in the text.

- ▶ This task is very similar to the summary, notes, table and flow chart completion tasks (see page 26). The difference is that each sentence is separate and there may be little or no connection between the topic of each question – the task may focus on completely separate pieces of information.

- ▶ Remember that your answers must be actual words and phrases that appear in the text. Do not try to think of different words and phrases that have the same meaning, because if you do this, your answer will be marked wrong, and you will lose marks unnecessarily.

- ▶ Read the instructions carefully. Notice how many words you can use to answer each question. The number of words may vary; you may be asked to write one, two or three words in each question. If you use more words, your answer will be wrong.

- ▶ The information required for this task may be in one specific section of the text or it may be spread throughout the text.

- ▶ See also page 70 for another type of sentence completion task.

Step-by-step guide

▶ **Step 1 – Locate the task in the text**

In this task, the title is very helpful. It tells you that the whole task is about a single topic discussed in the text, rather than about different topics spread throughout the text.

1 The title of the task refers to 'general causes'. In which paragraph of the text are 'general causes' described?

....

2 Does the next paragraph deal with 'general causes'? If not, what topic does it deal with?

....

▶ **Step 2 – Find the answers**

Look carefully at each sentence in the task and at the part of the text you identified in step 1.

Questions 2, 3 and *4* are all in one sentence in the task, and so it is likely that the answers to them will be quite close together in the text.

IELTS TEST 2

Exam Essentials

LISTENING MODULE   **READING MODULE**   WRITING MODULE   SPEAKING MODULE

PASSAGE 1
PASSAGE 2
PASSAGE 3

Step-by-step guide

(continued)

Question 2

The word 'both' after the gap indicates that the answer must have two parts.

1 The sentence in the task says that European countries 'kept' something. Which word in the text means 'kept' in this context?

....

2 Which word in the text means 'big'?

....

Now answer *Question 2*.

Question 3

The sentence in the task refers to something increasing. Which word in the text means 'increased' or 'higher' in the context?

....

Now answer *Question 3*.

Question 4

The sentence in the task indicates that the gap must be filled with something that people wanted to escape. Which word in the text means 'escape'?

....

Now answer *Question 4*.

Questions 5–9

Answer *Questions 5–9*, using the same process:

• Look at words and phrases before and after the gaps.

• Find words and phrases in the text that have similar meanings or express the same ideas in different ways.

• Find the exact word or phrase in the text that you must use as your answer.

Questions 10–13

Complete each sentence with the correct ending **A–H** *from the box below.*

Write the correct letter **A–H** *in boxes 10–13 on your answer sheet.*

10   The end of the potato famine in Ireland

11   People who had emigrated from Ireland

12   Movement off the land in the US

13   The arrival of railroad companies in the West of the US

> A   made people reluctant to move elsewhere.
>
> B   resulted in a need for more agricultural workers.
>
> C   provided evidence of the advantages of emigration.
>
> D   created a false impression of the advantages of moving elsewhere.
>
> E   did little to improve the position of much of the population.
>
> F   took a long time to have any real effect.
>
> G   failed to satisfy employment requirements.
>
> H   created a surplus of people who had emigrated.

Sentence completion (2)

Task guide

▸ This task requires you to choose which of the listed options correctly completes each sentence according to the information given in the text.

▸ This task may focus on a specific section or sections of the text or the information required for the question may be spread throughout the text.

▸ Questions in this task follow the order in which the relevant information appears in the text. For example, you will find the information required for *Question 13* after the information for *Question 12*.

▸ Some of the options do not correctly complete any of the sentences.

▸ Do not answer a question too quickly. It is very likely that more than one option will relate to the information required to complete a sentence, but only one option will match precisely what is stated in the text.

▸ See also page 69 for another type of sentence completion task.

Step-by-step guide

The best approach to this task is to:

• Look at the beginning of each sentence.
• Find the specific section of the text that relates to it.
• Read this section carefully and look through the options (A–H).
• Decide which one correctly matches the information in the text.

Question 10

▸ **Step 1 – Locate the question in the text**

1 Which paragraph mentions the potato famine in Ireland?

....

2 Find the sentence in that paragraph that refers to the end of the famine. Which phrase in that sentence means 'ended' or 'finished'?

....

▸ **Step 2 – Find the answer**

Look at the paragraph you identified in step 1. What does the writer say about the end of the famine?

A It made people want to stay in Ireland.

B It didn't really change the situation in Ireland.

C It eventually led to improvements in Ireland.

Look through the options (A–H) and choose the one that most closely matches your answer to this question.

Question 11

▸ **Step 1 – Locate the question in the text**

1 Which paragraph mentions people who had emigrated from Ireland?

....

2 In that paragraph, what word does the writer use to describe these people?

....

▸ **Step 2 – Find the answer**

Look at the sentence you identified in step 1. What does the writer say about people who had emigrated from Ireland?

A They told people at home about problems they were experiencing.

B They sent things home that indicated that their lives were good.

C They said their lives abroad were better than they really were.

Look through the options (A–H) and choose the one that most closely matches your answer to this question.

Questions 12–13

Answer *Questions 12–13*, using the same process:

• Find the part of the text that relates to the subject of the question.
• Consider carefully what is said in that part of the text.
• Find the option that matches what is said in the text.

IELTS
TEST 2

Exam Essentials

| LISTENING MODULE | READING MODULE | WRITING MODULE | SPEAKING MODULE |

PASSAGE 1
PASSAGE 2
PASSAGE 3

*You should spend about 20 minutes on **Questions 14–26**, which are based on Reading Passage 2 on pages 72 and 73.*

How bugs hitch-hike across the galaxy

Mankind's search for alien life could be jeopardised by ultra-resilient bacteria from Earth. David Derbyshire reports

What was the most important discovery of the Apollo programme? Some have argued that it was the rocks that explained how the Moon was formed. Others believe it was the technological spin-offs. But according to Captain Peter Conrad, who led the 1969 Apollo 12 mission, it was life.

On the apparently dead lunar surface, a colony of bacteria was thriving. The organisms were not native to the Moon, but were visitors from Earth who had hitch-hiked a ride on board one of Nasa's five Surveyor probes from the 1960s. To the astonishment of biologists, between 50 and 100 Streptococcus bacteria survived the journey across space, at an average temperature 20 degrees above absolute zero with no source of energy or water, and stayed alive on the Moon in a camera for three years. Captain Conrad, who returned the bacteria to Earth, was later to confess: 'I always thought the most significant thing we ever found on the whole Moon was the little bacteria that came back and lived.'

The ability of life to survive, adapt and evolve never fails to astonish. Over the past three decades, bacteria and archaea have been found in some of the most inhospitable places on Earth. Known as extremophiles, these organisms have coped with life in a vacuum, pressure as high as 70 tons per square inch, depths of four miles beneath the surface and scorching waters around deep-sea volcanic vents. They have also survived 25 million years inside a bee preserved in resin. Their resilience has renewed enthusiasm for the search for alien life – a quest that many had assumed had

been banished to fantasy fiction. Mars and the moons Titan, Europa and Callisto are once again plausible candidates for extraterrestrials.

As interest in alien life has grown, so have concerns that mankind could spread its own microscopic bugs, contaminating the places we want to explore. In 2003, Nasa ended the Galileo probe's mission by smashing it into Jupiter. The fear was that it could be carrying bacteria that might contaminate Europa's oceans.

The team behind Beagle 2 – the British probe that went to search for life on Mars in 2003 – was forced to take contamination particularly seriously. If Beagle carried to Mars life or dead spores picked up during the manufacture of the spacecraft, its science would be jeopardised. Prof Colin Pillinger, the Open University scientist who headed the Beagle project, said: 'What we've learnt since the Apollo missions and the Viking Mars missions of the 1970s is that bugs are far more tenacious than we ever imagined. They seem to be very tolerant of high temperatures, they lie dormant at low temperatures for long periods, they are immune to salt, acid and alkali, they seem to survive on substrate that are not what people expect. Extremophiles are extremely adapted to hanging on to life.'

Beagle had to be assembled in a 'clean room' – and one was specially put together in a converted BBC outside broadcast van garage in Milton Keynes. It had enough room to include an enormous set of fans that circulated and filtered the air 500 times an hour. Only a handful of trained researchers were allowed inside. 'I wasn't allowed in,' says Prof Pillinger. 'There was special training for people going in there and special conditions. There was a ban on beards and a limit of four people at any one time. The team kept samples of everything that could have contaminated the craft and monitored every stage of assembly.'

To reduce the workload, the idea was to build as much as possible before sterilising it and banishing it to the difficult working conditions inside the clean room. The easy stuff was heated to 115C for 52 hours, more than enough to kill off bugs. Electronic equipment can't cope with those sorts of temperatures, so the team used a hydrogen peroxide plasma, created in a microwave, to kill off bugs at low temperatures. Parachutes and gas bags were zapped with gamma radiation. It wasn't just facial hair that was banned. 'You've heard of the paperless office,' says Prof Pillinger. 'We had the paperless assembly line. The guys normally go in armed with loads of papers and diagrams, but we didn't allow any of that. They were given information through a glass wall, over mikes and monitors. And sometimes on a piece of paper stuck to the glass with sticky tape.'

Beagle's heat shield doubled as its biological shield. So once the instruments were encased and sealed, the craft could be brought back into the real world. The shield heated up to 1,700 degrees on its descent through the Martian atmosphere, so bugs on the casing were not a worry. Mars Express – the craft carrying Beagle – did not need sterilising. Its trajectory was designed so that if something went wrong, the craft would not simply crash into the planet. Its course could be corrected en route.

Eventually, space scientists hope to return samples of Mars to Earth. While the risks of alien bacteria proving hazardous on Earth may be remote, the rocks will still need to be quarantined. Moon rocks from Apollo were analysed in vacuum glove boxes for the first two missions. Later, researchers stored rocks in nitrogen. Prof Pillinger believed the first Mars rocks should be sterilised before they are studied on Earth. 'For security purposes it would be the most sensible thing to do. You don't have to sterilise it all, you can contain some of it and then sterilise the sample you want to look at, but it would lower the risk and make it easier to analyse.'

IELTS
TEST 2

Exam Essentials

LISTENING MODULE	READING MODULE	WRITING MODULE	SPEAKING MODULE

PASSAGE 1
PASSAGE 2
PASSAGE 3

Questions 14–20

*Look at the statements (**Questions 14–20**) and the list of spacecraft below.*

Match each statement with the spacecraft it applies to.

*Write the correct letter **A–E** in boxes 14–20 on your answer sheet.*

14   provided transport from Earth for bacteria

15   led to realisation of how tenacious bacteria are

16   was created so that there could be no bacteria on the outer structure

17   was capable of changing direction in the event of a problem

18   brought material which was kept in more than one kind of container

19   required action because of the possibility of the introduction of harmful bacteria

20   resulted in disagreement as to the relative value of what was found

---

List of Spacecraft

A   Apollo craft

B   Surveyor probe

C   Galileo probe

D   Beagle 2

E   Mars Express

Matching statements to options

Task guide

▶ This task requires you to match statements with the people or things in the text that they apply to. For example, you may be required to decide which people in the text express the views presented in the questions, or you may be required to decide which thing, place, creature, etc. in a text each statement is true of.

▶ Make sure that the option you choose matches precisely what is stated in the text. Sometimes a statement may relate in some way to more than one option, but it will only match one option precisely.

▶ This task is very similar to classification tasks (see page 42). The difference is that in this task the options are people or things, whereas in classification tasks the options are categories.

▶ See also pages 28 and 34 for other types of matching tasks.

Step-by-step guide

The best approach to this task is to:

• identify the section where each of the options is mentioned

• focus on these parts of the text, rather than constantly looking through the whole text and

• look at each question one by one and find the relevant part of the text.

▸ **Step 1 – Locate the options in the text**

In which paragraphs of the text are there references to each of the options (A–E)?

A Apollo ....

B Surveyor ....

C Galileo ....

D Beagle ....

E Mars Express ....

▸ **Step 2 – Find the answers**

This task involves more than simply matching words and phrases in the statements with words and phrases that mean the same in the text. Some questions involve finding the part of the text which presents the same idea as that contained in the question.

Question 14

Look through the parts of the text you identified in step 1. You are looking for a reference to bacteria being transported from Earth.

1 Which paragraph contains this reference?

....

Look at the paragraph you identified and answer this question.

2 Which phrase in this paragraph means 'was given a lift'?

....

Decide which spacecraft (A–E) this applies to and answer *Question 14*.

Question 15

Look through the parts of the text you identified in Step 1. You are looking for a reference to bacteria being tenacious.

1 What does 'tenacious' mean in this context?
   A moving quickly
   B very strong
   C easy to destroy

2 Which paragraph contains a reference to this characteristic?

....

Look at the paragraph you identified above and answer these questions:

3 What kind of bacteria was it?

....

4 Who was on the spacecaft which found it?

....

Decide which spacecraft (A–E) this person was on and answer *Question 15*.

Questions 16–20

Now answer *Questions 16–20*, using the same process:

• Look at each question and look through the parts of the text you identified in step 1 to find the place in the text that relates to each statement.

• When you have found that place, identify which spacecraft is referred to.

IELTS
TEST **2**

Exam Essentials

LISTENING MODULE   **READING MODULE**   WRITING MODULE   SPEAKING MODULE

PASSAGE 1
PASSAGE 2
PASSAGE 3

Questions 21–26

Label the diagram below.

Choose **NO MORE THAN THREE WORDS** *from the reading passage for each answer.*

Write your answers in boxes 21–26 on your answer sheet.

THE ASSEMBLY OF BEAGLE 2

spacecraft built in newly created **21** ....

22 ....

large number of **26** ....

bacteria on **23** ....
destroyed at low temperatures

24 ....

parachutes and gas bags

people not allowed to have **25** ....

Labelling a diagram

Task guide

▸ This task requires you to complete descriptions of a diagram using words that appear in the text. Remember to use words and phrases that actually appear in the text. Do not try to think of different words or phrases with the same meaning.

▸ The information you require will normally appear in one specific part of the text.

▸ Within that part of the text, the information may not appear in the same order as the question numbers in the diagram. The questions usually begin at the top left of the diagram and go round in a clockwise direction. It is therefore essential to keep looking carefully at the diagram and the parts that you need to label so that you do not get confused about the order.

Step-by-step guide

▶ **Step 1 – Locate the task in the text**

Look for clues in the title of the diagram (if there is one) or in the questions on the diagram. In this case, the title ('The Assembly of Beagle 2') points you to the relevant part of the text.

1 The relevant part of the text begins with a reference to Beagle being 'assembled'. In which paragraph and in which sentence in that paragraph is this reference?

....

2 Where does the description of the assembly of Beagle end in the text?

....

▶ **Step 2 – Find the answers**

The best approach is to look at each question in number order and then find the relevant information in the text.

Remember that the order of the questions may not be the same as the order in which the information appears in the text. If you try to take a different approach, beginning with what is said in the text and then finding which question it refers to, you may become confused and put answers into the wrong gaps.

Before looking through the text, make sure that you are clear about exactly what is being labelled.

Question 21

The arrow indicates that it refers to the whole place where Beagle was assembled.

The question tells you that you are looking for a place that was 'newly created', not one that previously existed.

Read the parts of the text you identified in step 1. Which phrase in the text means 'newly created'?

....

Identify the place that was newly created and answer *Question 21*.

Question 22

The arrow indicates that something that separated one place from another must be labelled.

Look through the parts of the text you identified in step 1. Communication took place from one side of this object to the other. What three things are mentioned as methods of communication?

....

Identify this dividing object and answer *Question 22*.

Questions 23–25

Now answer *Questions 23–25*, using the same process:

• Look at each question in number order.

• Make sure you are clear as to exactly what is being labelled.

• Look for the relevant information in the text.

• Use any other words in the label to help you find the relevant information in the text.

IELTS TEST 2

Exam Essentials

LISTENING MODULE   READING MODULE   WRITING MODULE   SPEAKING MODULE

PASSAGE 1
PASSAGE 2
PASSAGE 3

*You should spend about 20 minutes on **Questions 27–40**, which are based on Reading Passage 3 on pages 78 and 79.*

Finding out about the world from television news

In The Ideological Octopus (1991), Justin Lewis points to an important issue concerning the formal structure of television news. As he notes, television news lacks the narrative element which, in other genres, serves to capture viewer interest and thus motivate viewing. Lewis posits this as one of the key reasons why television news often fails to interest people and why, when they do watch it, people often cannot understand it. Lewis argues that one fundamental problem with watching television news is that its narrative structure means that the viewer is offered the punchline before the joke – because the main point (the headline) comes right at the beginning, after which the programme, by definition, deals with less and less important things. Thus, in television news our interest is not awakened by an enigma which is then gradually solved, to provide a gratifying solution – as so often happens in fictional narratives. In Lewis's terms, in television news there is no enigma, the solution of which will motivate the viewing process. As he baldly states, 'If we decided to try to design a television programme with a structure that would completely fail to capture an audience's interest, we might (finally) come up with the format of the average television news show' (Lewis 1991).

What Lewis also does is offer an interesting contrast, in this respect, between the high-status phenomenon of television news and the low-status genre of soap opera. The latter, he observes, offers the most highly developed use of effective narrative codes. To that extent soap opera, with its multiple narratives, could be seen, in formal terms, as the most effective type of television for the cultivation of viewer interest, and certainly as a far more effective form than that of television news for this purpose. Clearly, some of Lewis's speculation here is problematic. There are counter-examples of his arguments (e.g. instances of programmes such as sports news which share the problematic formal features he points to but which are nonetheless popular – at least among certain types of viewers). Moreover, he may perhaps overstress the importance of structure as against content relevance in providing the basis for

programme appeal. Nonetheless, I would suggest that his argument, in this respect, is of considerable interest.

Lewis argues not only that soap opera is more narratively interesting than television news, in formal terms, but, moreover, that the world of television fiction in general is much closer to most people's lives than that presented in the news. This, he claims, is because the world of television fiction often feels to people like their own lives. They can, for example, readily identify with the moral issues and personal dilemmas faced by the characters in a favourite soap opera. Conversely, the world of television news is much more remote in all senses; it is a socially distant world populated by another race of special or 'elite' persons, the world of 'them' not 'us'. This is also why 'most people feel more able to evaluate TV fiction than TV news ... because it seems closer to their own lives and to the world they live in ... [whereas] the world of television news ... might almost be beamed in from another planet' (Lewis 1991). It is as if the distant world of 'the news' is so disconnected from popular experience that it is beyond critical judgement for many viewers. Hence, however alienated they feel from it, they nonetheless lack any alternative perspective on the events it portrays.

One consequence of this, Lewis argues, is that precisely, because of this distance, people who feel this kind of alienation from the 'world of news' nonetheless use frameworks to understand news items which come from within the news themselves. This, he argues, is because in the absence of any other source of information or perspective they are forced back on using the media's own framework. Many viewers are simply unable to place the media's portrayal of events in any other critical framework (where would they get it from?). To this extent, Lewis argues, Gerbner and his colleagues (see Gerbner et al. 1986; Signorielli and Morgan 1990) may perhaps be right in thinking that the dominant perspectives and 'associative logics' offered by the media may often simply be soaked up by audiences by sheer dint of their repetition. This is not to suggest that such viewers necessarily believe, or explicitly accept, these perspectives, but simply to note that they have no other place to start from, however cynical they may be, at a general level, about 'not believing what you see on television', and they may thus tend, in the end, to fall back on 'what it said on TV'. In one sense, this could be said to be the converse of Hall's 'negotiated code' (1980), as taken over from Parkin (1973). Parkin had argued that many working-class people display a 'split consciousness', whereby they accept propositions from the 'dominant ideology' at an abstract level, but then 'negotiate' or 'discount' the application of these ideological propositions to the particular circumstances of their own situation. Here, by contrast, we confront a situation where people often express cynicism in general (so that 'not believing what you see in the media' is no more than common sense), but then in any particular case they often find themselves pushed back into reliance on the mainstream media's account of anything beyond the realm of their direct personal experience, simply for lack of any alternative perspective.

IELTS TEST 2

Exam Essentials

| LISTENING MODULE | READING MODULE | WRITING MODULE | SPEAKING MODULE |

PASSAGE 1
PASSAGE 2
PASSAGE 3

Questions 27–34

Complete the summary below using words from the box.

Write your answers in boxes 27–34 on your answer sheet.

The structure of television news

Justin Lewis says that television news does not have the **27** .... feature that other types of programme have.

As a result, many viewers do not find it interesting and may find it **28** .... . This is because the **29** ....

information comes first and after that **30** .... matters are covered. In television news, there is no **31** ....

progress towards a conclusion and nothing **32** .... to find out about. In fact, he believes that television news

is an example of how the **33** .... process in the field of television could result in something that is **34** .... to

what constitutes an interesting programme.

upsetting	creative	secondary	controversial	fast-moving
contrary	opinionated	routine	step-by-step	informal
crucial	story-telling	additional	overwhelming	mysterious
repetitive	informative	related	confusing	diverse

Summary completion (with choices)

Task guide

▶ This task requires you to fill in gaps in a summary with the correct words that appear in the box.

▶ This task usually, but not always, focusses on one particular part or section of the text, rather than on information that is spread throughout the text.

▶ The words in the box will normally all belong to the same part of speech (adjectives, nouns, etc.). You are therefore required to decide on the word with the correct meaning for each gap, not what kind of word fits grammatically.

▶ The words you need to choose have the same or very similar meanings to words and phrases used in the text, or they express the same ideas as what is stated in the text.

▶ The questions follow the same order as the relevant information in the text.

▶ There are significantly more words to choose from in the box than there are answers. Be careful. Several words in the box may be connected in meaning, but only one will have the precise meaning required to match what is stated in the text.

▶ See also page 26 for another type of summary completion task.

Step-by-step guide

First of all, you need to identify which words and phrases in the text relate to each gap. Then you need to find the word in the box that has the same meaning as those words or phrases, or expresses the same idea as what is stated in the text.

▸ Step 1 – Locate the task in the text

In this case, the title and the reference to Justin Lewis at the beginning of the summary can help you locate the task in the text.

Which sentence in the text contains a reference to the structure of television news and Justin Lewis?

....

▸ Step 2 – Find the answers

As with the summary task that does not have a box of choices (see page 26), the summary in this task presents the information and ideas in the text in different words and phrases from those in the text. You will need to understand the ideas that are contained in the text and see how they relate to the content of the summary.

The box contains words that mean the same as words or ideas that appear in the text. To answer each question, you first need to identify which part of the text relates to the gap in the summary. Then you must identify the word in the box that has the same meaning as the relevant word or idea in the text.

Question 27

1 Look at the words before and after the gap, and look at the part of the text you identified in step 1. Which word in the text means 'feature' in this context?

....

2 The summary refers to other types of programme. Which word in the text means 'types'?

....

3 You are looking for a feature that television news doesn't have, but other types of programme do have. Which word in the text means 'doesn't have'?

....

4 Which word in the text could fill the gap in the summary?

....

Now look at the words in the box and find the word that has the same meaning as this word from the text.

Now write your answer for *Question 27*.

Question 28

Look at the paragraph you identified in step 1.

The sentence containing the gap in the summary refers to two reactions that viewers have to television news. One is that they don't find it interesting. What other problem does the text say that they have?

....

Question 28 relates to the phrase you have just identified. Now look at the words in the box and find the word that expresses the same idea.

Now write your answer for *Question 28*.

Questions 29–34

Answer *Questions 29–34*, using the same process:

• Look at the words before and after each gap and find the part of the text that relates to them.

• Find a word in the text that could fill the gap or identify a phrase in the text that expresses the idea of the word that fills the gap.

• Look through the box of choices and identify the word that matches the meaning of the word in the text or expresses the same idea as the phrase in the text.

IELTS TEST 2

Exam Essentials

LISTENING MODULE   **READING MODULE**   WRITING MODULE   SPEAKING MODULE

PASSAGE 1
PASSAGE 2
PASSAGE 3

Questions 35–40

Do the following statements agree with the information given in Reading Passage 3?

In boxes 35–40 on your answer sheet write

> **TRUE**   *if the statement agrees with the information.*
>
> **FALSE**   *if the statement contradicts the information.*
>
> **NOT GIVEN**   *if there is no information on this.*

35   Lewis concentrates more on the structure of programmes than on what is actually in them.

36   Lewis regrets viewers' preference for soap operas over television news.

37   Lewis suggests that viewers sometimes find that television news contradicts their knowledge of the world.

38   Lewis believes that viewers have an inconsistent attitude towards the reliability of television news.

39   Parkin states that many working class people see themselves as exceptions to general beliefs.

40   The writer of the text believes that viewers should have a less passive attitude towards what they are told by the media.

True/False/Not Given

Task guide

▶ This task, which is very similar to the Yes/No/Not Given task (see page 36), tests you on the detailed understanding of complex pieces of information in the text.

▶ For an answer to be 'False', there must be something in the text that makes the statement in the question definitely incorrect.

▶ Questions to which the answer is 'Not Given' involve something being stated in the text that relates to the statement in the question, but which does not actually match the statement or directly show it to be correct or incorrect.

▶ The questions follow the order in which the relevant information appears in the text.

▶ This task may focus on one specific part of the text, but it is more likely that the information relevant to it will be spread throughout the text or large parts of it.

Step-by-step guide

The best approach to this task is to:

- look at each question one by one
- find the relevant part of the text
- study the question and that part of the text carefully and
- decide on your answer.

Remember that you will have to understand the ideas presented in the text, and that you may not find words and phrases in the text that mean the same as those in the question.

▸ Step 1 – Locate the task in the text

This is a very difficult text. Before starting the task, it is a good idea to locate the task in the text.

1 *Question 35* refers to 'structure'. Which paragraph(s) of the text mention the structure of programmes?

....

2 *Question 36* mentions 'soap operas'. Which paragraph(s) of the text refer to soap operas?

....

3 *Question 39* refers to Parkin. In which paragraph is Parkin mentioned?

....

4 Where do you think you will find the answers to this task?
   A in one specific part of the text
   B spread throughout the text

▸ Step 2 – Find the answers

As with the Yes/No/Not Given task (see page 36), to answer the questions you will need to find the relevant part of the text, read it carefully and ask yourself three questions:

- Is the same thing stated in the text?
- Is the opposite stated in the text?
- Is there no information on this particular matter in the text?

Question 35

1 Find a sentence in the text that mentions that Lewis concentrates more on one thing than another. What is the first word of that sentence?

....

2 Which phrase in that sentence means 'concentrate too much on' or 'put too much emphasis on'?

....

3 In that sentence, which word means 'what is in something'?

....

Now answer *Question 35*.

Question 36

1 Find a paragraph that deals with why people prefer soap operas but doesn't deal with the differences in structure between soap operas and television news.

....

2 Read this paragraph carefully. Does Lewis say that he can understand why people prefer soap operas?

....

3 Does Lewis say that he also prefers soap operas to television news?

....

4 Does Lewis say that he prefers television news to soap operas?

....

Now answer *Question 36*.

Questions 37–40

Answer *Questions 37–40*, using the same process:

- Find the part of the text that relates to the question.
- Read carefully what is stated in that part of the text and in the question.
- Ask yourself the three questions at the beginning of step 2.

You should spend about 20 minutes on this task.

The table below gives information about the five small companies in Britain that came top in a survey of staff conducted by a national newspaper to find out which companies are the best to work for.

Summarise the information by selecting and reporting the main features, and make comparisons where relevant.

Write at least 150 words.

THE FIVE BEST SMALL COMPANIES TO WORK FOR

POSITION IN SURVEY	1ST	2ND	3RD	4TH	5TH
staff numbers	56	79	72	76	190
male:female ratio	30:70	47:53	74:26	13:87	51:49
under 35s / over 55s	77% / 0%	59% / 1%	82% / 0%	26% / 8%	93% / 0%
staff turnover	5%	18%	8%	13%	33%
staff in high income bracket	34%	48%	74%	5%	2%

Describing tables

Task guide

▶ Many Task 1 questions involve tables presented in columns, according to categories, etc.

▶ A task may involve a single table, more than one table, or a table together with a bar chart or graph.

▶ This task involves a single table with data on five companies in five categories.

▶ For this kind of task, you must select important information and summarise it. Do not list all the data presented in the table.

▶ Make sure that you include all relevant points. If important information is missing from your answer, you may lose marks.

▶ Look for overall patterns or trends. It is possible, however, that there are no simple patterns or obvious general trends. If this is the case, you could say this in your answer.

▶ Remember that your answer must not be too short or too long. It is better to write just over 150 words and check that your answer flows well and logically, and that the English is accurate, than to write a longer answer.

▶ Remember that tasks in the Writing module will be marked according to certain criteria:
Content: Have you included all the relevant information?
Organisation: Does your answer flow well and is it clear and easy to read?
Use of language: Have you used appropriate linking words and phrases? Have you used a range of grammatical structures? Is the vocabulary used accurately?

Step-by-step guide

▶ **Step 1 – Find the main point(s)**

1 Look carefully through the table. What do you notice?

A The company that came first is different from all the others in every category.

B There are differences between the five companies in every category.

C None of the companies have anything in common with each other.

2

a What is the highest number of staff and which company has it?

....

b What is the lowest number of staff and which company has it?

....

3

a How many companies have more male than female staff?

....

b Which company has the highest proportion of female staff?

....

4

a What is the highest percentage of staff aged under 35 and which company has it?

....

b What is the highest percentage of staff aged over 55 among the five companies and which company has it?

....

5 How many companies have a staff turnover rate of over 10%?

....

6 How many companies have fewer than 10% of staff earning high incomes?

....

▶ **Step 2 – Organise your answer**

1 What should you begin your answer with?

A a description of the company that came first

B a reference to whether there is a general pattern or not

C a comparison of the staff numbers in the various companies

2 What should come next?

A a sentence or sentences about each category

B a sentence or sentences about each company

C a comment on each one of the figures

▶ **Step 3 – Language to use**

Write a sentence based on the information in the table, using one word or phrase from each of these lists:

Linking phrases

• *apart from, except for*
• *as for, with regard to*

....
....

Grammatical structures: adverbs

greatly, fairly, comparatively, far, extremely

....
....

Vocabulary: difference and similarity

have in common with, differ from, be similar to, difference between

....
....

Use your answers for step 1, 2 and 3 to plan your answer.

Now write your answer for Task 1.

There is a sample answer on page 200.

You should spend about 40 minutes on this task.

Present a written argument or case to an educated reader with no specialist knowledge of the following topic.

> *The ease of international travel and the spread of various kinds of mass media all over the world have made it more possible than ever for people to know how other people live in other countries.*
>
> *Do the advantages of this development outweigh the disadvantages?*

You should use your own ideas, knowledge and experience and support your arguments with examples and relevant evidence. Write at least 250 words.

Giving your opinion (2)

Task guide

▸ Remember to read the statement(s) and the question very carefully, so that you do exactly what you are asked to do in your answer.

▸ Some tasks ask you to discuss the advantages and disadvantages of something, while others ask you to discuss the causes of a problem and suggest possible solutions to it. In tasks of this type, you may be asked the following questions:
  (a) *Do the advantages of this outweigh the disadvantages?*
  (b) *Do you think this is a positive or negative development?*
  (c) *What do you think are the causes of this problem and what measures could be taken to solve/reduce it?*

  In this case, Task 2 is an example of (a). There are examples of (b) and (c) in other tests in this book.

▸ Remember to concentrate on presenting a clear and logical argument that the reader can follow easily.

▸ Remember to divide your answer into paragraphs appropriately.

▸ Remember that your answer must not be too short or too long.

▸ Remember that tasks in the Writing module will be assessed according to certain criteria:

  Content: Have you included all the relevant information?
  Organisation: Does your answer flow well and is it clear and easy to read?
  Use of language: Have you used appropriate linking words and phrases? Have you used a range of grammatical structures? Is the vocabulary used accurately?

Step-by-step guide

▶ **Step 1 – Read the question carefully**

Look at Task 2. Which FIVE of the following should you do in your answer?

1 Compare international travel now and in the past.

2 Discuss the effect of international travel on local economies and the environment.

3 Discuss relationships between visitors and local people.

4 Compare the quality of different types of mass media.

5 Give examples of types of mass media that have spread.

6 Discuss the reactions people have when seeing programmes about other countries.

7 Give examples of political events that have been covered by media all over the world.

8 Give an opinion on whether developments in travel and mass media have been beneficial in life in general.

9 Give an opinion on whether developments in travel and mass media have affected relationships between different nationalities.

▶ **Step 2 – Organise your answer**

Using your answers for step 1, make a plan for your answer:

• Deal with each of the two topics – international travel and mass media – separately.

• Discuss the developments and advantages of each separately.

• Then discuss the disadvantages of both of them together.

• Finally, present a conclusion.

This is a suggested plan only. You could decide to organise your answer in a different way.

Now write your notes:

International travel

Developments: ....

....

Advantages: ....

....

Mass media

Developments: ....

....

Advantages: ....

....

International travel – disadvantages

....

Mass media – disadvantages

....

Conclusion

....

▶ **Step 3 – Language to use**

Using your notes for step 2, write a sentence using one word or phrase from each of these lists:

Linking words and phrases
• *first of all, in addition, in conclusion, on the whole*
• *because, as, since, as a result*
• *although, though, whereas*

....

....

....

Grammatical structures
• comparison: *more ... than, less ... than*
• clauses beginning with *what* and *how*
• reflexives: *themselves, each other, one another*

....

....

....

Vocabulary
• *affordable, accessible*
• *envy, envious, sympathy, sympathetic, understanding*
• *cause, lead to, create, produce*

....

....

....

Now write your answer for Task 2.

There is a sample answer on page 200.

IELTS TEST 2

Exam Essentials

LISTENING MODULE   READING MODULE   WRITING MODULE   **SPEAKING MODULE**

PART 1
PART 2
PART 3

Assessment guide

In the Speaking module, the examiner will assess your performance on the basis of:

- Fluency and coherence
- Lexical resource
- Grammatical range and accuracy
- Pronunciation

The examiner will be applying these four criteria at all times in all three parts of the Speaking module.

Fluency and coherence
This refers to how much and quickly you speak, and to how organised what you say is. If you pause a lot, or repeat yourself, you do not communicate very effectively. If you talk reasonably continuously, and present what you say in a logical and organised way, you communicate well.

Lexical resource
This refers to the vocabulary you use. If you understand what you are asked, you will be able to answer the

examiner's questions effectively. If you are able to use a variety of words and expressions to say what you want, you will be interesting to listen to.

Grammatical range and accuracy
This refers to the grammar you use. If you only use simple structures and do not vary them, you will not be very interesting to listen to. But if you do not make a large number of mistakes, and you also use different structures, then you will be able to communicate what you want to say effectively.

Pronunciation
This refers to the way you pronounce individual sounds, words, phrases and complete sections of talk. For example, if you do not pronounce certain sounds distinctly, or if you don't use the intonation patterns of the English language, it can be difficult for the examiner to understand what you are saying. If all aspects of your pronunciation are clear and correct, the examiner will be able to understand what you want to say easily.

Part 1 – Example questions

What journeys do you make every day?
What do you do during journeys?
Do you sometimes have problems with transport?
What is your favourite form of transport?

Step-by-step guide

▶ **Step 1 – Check your grammar**

Look at this candidate's answer for this task.

Examiner: What journeys do you make every day?
Candidate: I go college every day. I go by foot to underground station and take a train for about 15 minutes.
Examiner: What do you do during journeys?
Candidate: Sometimes I reading a newspaper, but if I travel with my friend we will talk a lot.
Examiner: Do you sometimes have problems with transport?
Candidate: The trains have crowded, and sometimes are delay and I arrive to college late.
Examiner: What is your favourite form of transport?
Candidate: I like planes best. They are very fast and convenient, despite expensive.

How would you assess this candidate's grammar? Has the candidate used a good range of structures? Can you find any mistakes?

▶ **Step 2 – Improve your answer**

Look at the candidate's answer again. Correct the mistakes by filling in some of the gaps with words from the box.

are	at	being	delayed	on	read	the	to

I go **1** .... college every day. I go **2** .... foot to **3** .... underground station and take a train for about 15 minutes.

Sometimes I **4** .... a newspaper, but if I travel with my friend, we **5** .... talk a lot.

The trains **6** .... crowded, and sometimes are **7** ...., and I arrive **8** .... college late.

I like **9** .... planes best. They are very fast and convenient, despite **10** .... expensive.

Part 2 – Example questions

Read the topic card below carefully. You will have to talk about the topic for one to two minutes.

You have one minute to think about what you are going to say.

You can make notes to help you if you wish.

> Describe a conversation you had which was important to you.
>
> You should say:
>
> - when the conversation took place
> - who you had the conversation with
> - what the conversation was about
>
> and explain why the conversation was important to you.

Step-by-step guide

▸ Step 1 – Check for fluency and coherence

Look at the candidate's notes and answer for this task.

- 3 years ago – visiting my parents
- George – my uncle
- going to England
- changed my life

I remember one conversation that was important to me. It was about three years ago, and it had a big impact on my life. What happened was that my uncle – George, he is my mother's brother, and lives in London – he has a business – talked to me. He was visiting us in my country. I was bored with my life, and I was complaining about how I didn't know what to do – there aren't many opportunities in my small town, you see. My uncle said that I should come to London. He could help me to find work and meet people. Then I could study and get qualifications. I did it and I came to London. Now I have a job and I study part–time. This conversation changed my life. Without this conversation, I would still be bored at home.

How would you assess this candidate's fluency and coherence? Can you find any areas that need improvement?

▸ Step 2 – Improve your answer

Look at the candidate's answer again. Improve the fluency and coherence by filling in the gaps with words from the box.

a at the time
b in particular
c so
d this was because
e what he suggested
f where
g who
h would be able to

I remember one conversation **1** …….. that was important to me. It was about three years ago, and it had a big impact on my life. What happened was that my uncle – George, **2** …….. is my mother's brother, and lives in London **3** …….. he has a business – talked to me. He was visiting us in my country. **4** …….. I was bored with my life, and I was complaining about how I didn't know what to do – **5** …….. there aren't many opportunities in my small town, you see. My uncle said that I should come to London. He could help me to find work and meet people. Then I **6** …….. study and get qualifications. I did **7** …….. and **8** …….. I came to London. Now I have a job and I study part-time. This conversation changed my life. Without this conversation, I would still be bored at home.

IELTS TEST 2

Exam Essentials

LISTENING MODULE   READING MODULE   WRITING MODULE   **SPEAKING MODULE**

PART 1
PART 2
PART 3

Part 3 – Example questions

A   What differences are there when using channels of communication (face-to-face, telephone, writing)?

B   To what extent do you think films and TV influence how people communicate with each other?

C   Do you think that there are differences in the way men and women communicate?

D   Do you agree that education has a strong and positive effect on people's ability to communicate effectively?

E   What impact do you think the growth of technology might have on communication in the future?

Step-by-step guide

▸ **Step 1 – Check your vocabulary**

Look at this candidate's answer for this task.

Examiner: What factors need to be considered when using different channels of communication (face-to-face, telephone, writing)?

Candidate: Well, for example, when you're talking on the telephone, you can't see the other person so you have to depend on your voice. When you're writing, you have more time to think about what you want to say, but on the other hand, if the other person doesn't understand, they can't ask you to say what you mean.

Examiner: To what extent do you think films and TV influence how people communicate with each other?

Candidate: I think that's something that's very hard to know. But we watch a large amount of TV from the US, for example, and people tend to copy expressions and attitudes of the actors.

Examiner: Do you think that there are differences in the way men and women communicate?

Candidate: I'm not sure … people say there are. Personally, I think that there might be more important differences, across cultures, for example. Or generations – the way old and young people communicate.

Examiner: Do you agree that education has a strong and positive effect on people's ability to communicate effectively?

Candidate: I would say that it can do, that it should do. It can increase your awareness of things beyond your own direct experience, and so make you better at communicating. On the other hand, a lot of education is very specialised and separate from daily life.

Examiner: What impact do you think the growth of technology might have on communication in the future?

Candidate: I'm afraid that it won't be good. We are likely to become more and more isolated, sitting over computers, sending emails rather than meeting and talking together properly.

How would you assess the candidate's vocabulary? Has the candidate used a range of different words and expressions? Are they used correctly?

Step-by-step guide

(continued)

▶ **Step 2 – Use alternatives**

Look at the candidate's answer again. There are gaps and there are possible answers. Choose the word from the box for each gap that will fit in with what the candidate says.

beneficial	calculate	claim	clarify	considerable
consider	develop	hunched	imitate	increasingly
immediate	rely	remote	significant	suspect

A Well, for example, when you're talking on the telephone, you can't see the other person so you have to **1** …….. on your voice. When you're writing, you have more time to **2** …….. what you want to say, but on the other hand, if the other person doesn't understand, they can't ask you to **3** …….. what you mean.

B I think that's something that's very hard to **1** …….. . But we watch a **2** …….. amount of TV from the US, for example, and people tend to **3** …….. expressions and attitudes of the actors.

C I'm not sure – people **1** …….. there are. Personally, I **2** …….. that there might be more **3** …….. differences, across cultures, for example. Or generations – the way old and young people communicate.

D I would say that it can do, that it should do. It can **1** …….. your awareness of things beyond your own **2** …….. experience, and so make you better at communicating. On the other hand, a lot of education is very specialised and **3** …….. from daily life.

E I'm afraid that it won't be **1** …….. . We are likely to become **2** …….. isolated, **3**…….. over computers, sending emails rather than meeting and talking together properly.

▶ **Questions 1–10**

Answer the questions below.

Write **NO MORE THAN THREE WORDS AND/OR A NUMBER** *for each answer.*

1   How many members does the cycling club have currently?

....

2   How much does Youth Membership cost?

....

3   From whom must you get a signature when applying to join?

....

4   How long does it take to process a membership application?

....

5   How often do family rides take place?

....

6   How long are the Saturday rides usually?

....

7   What must you get for your bike?

....

8   When is the next camping tour?

....

9   What is happening on May 5th?

....

10   How much discount do members get at Wheels Bike Shop?

....

SECTION 1
SECTION 2
SECTION 3
SECTION 4

▶ *Questions 11–20*

Complete the timetable below.

Write **NO MORE THAN THREE WORDS AND/OR A NUMBER** *for each answer.*

PARK ARTS CENTRE

DATES	TIMES	EVENT	NOTES
18 – 24 Feb	**11** .... and	Folk music concert	Can get a **12** .... in shop
1 – 8 March	See the **13**	Annual **14**	Groups from **15** ....
16	8pm	Film: **17** ' .... '	Talk by the **18** ....
2 April	To be confirmed	**19**	It will be **20** ....

LISTENING MODULE   READING MODULE   WRITING MODULE   SPEAKING MODULE

SECTION 1
SECTION 2
SECTION 3
SECTION 4

▸ **Questions 21–30**

Questions 21–25

What opinion is expressed about each dissertation?

Choose your answers from the box and write the letters **A–I** *next to questions 21–25.*

A	It has an inadequate index.
B	It contains unusual illustrations.
C	It is too detailed in places.
D	It presents clear arguments.
E	It contains diagrams which are not clear.
F	It omits important historical facts.
G	It is poorly translated.
H	It contains useful background information.
I	It is not suitable for new students.

21 Twentieth Century Architecture   ....
22 Modern Construction   ....
23 Steel, Glass and Concrete   ....
24 The Space We Make   ....
25 Change and Tradition   ....

Questions 26–30

Complete the flow chart below.

Write **NO MORE THAN THREE WORDS** *for each answer.*

BEN'S PROGRAMME

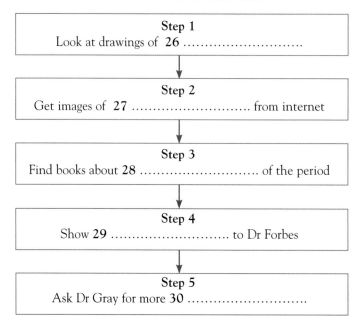

> **Step 1**
> Look at drawings of 26 ....

> **Step 2**
> Get images of 27 .... from internet

> **Step 3**
> Find books about 28 .... of the period

> **Step 4**
> Show 29 .... to Dr Forbes

> **Step 5**
> Ask Dr Gray for more 30 ....

LISTENING MODULE   READING MODULE   WRITING MODULE   SPEAKING MODULE

SECTION 1
SECTION 2
SECTION 3
SECTION 4

▶ **Questions 31–40**

Complete the sentences below.

Write **NO MORE THAN TWO WORDS** *for each answer.*

31   Rival cameras were claimed to ………………………….. less than the Cinématographe.

32   In Russia, on one occasion, the Cinématographe was suspected of being a ……………………………… .

33   Early filming in Russia led to the creation of a new approach to ……………………………… .

34   One problem for historians is not knowing whether early equipment ……………………………….. as it was claimed.

35   Marey encountered difficulties achieving the ……………………………….. of strips of photographic paper.

36   The ……………………………….. of the comic strip influenced the way films were planned.

37   Documentaries used ……………………………….. shots before fiction films did.

38   The popularity of ……………………………….. films led to increased numbers of shots.

39   When filming ……………………………….. , the screen might be divided.

40   As films became more complex, ……………………………….. became an important part of film-making.

IELTS TEST 3
Exam Essentials

LISTENING MODULE | READING MODULE | WRITING MODULE | SPEAKING MODULE
PASSAGE 1
PASSAGE 2
PASSAGE 3

*You should spend about 20 minutes on **Questions 1–13**, which are based on Reading Passage 1 on pages 96 and 97.*

Working in the movies

When people ask French translator Virginie Verdier what she does for a living, it must be tempting to say enigmatically: 'Oh me? I'm in the movies'. It's strictly true, but her starring role is behind the scenes. As translating goes, it doesn't get more entertaining or glamorous than subtitling films. If you're very lucky, you get to work on the new blockbuster films before they're in the cinema, and if you're just plain lucky, you get to work on the blockbuster movies that are going to video or DVD.

Virginie is quick to point out that this is as exacting as any translating job. 'You work hard. It's not all entertainment as you are doing the translating. You need all the skills of a good translator and those of a top-notch editor. You have to be precise and, of course, much more concise than in traditional translation work.'

The process starts when you get the original script and a tape. 'We would start with translating and adapting the film script. The next step is what we call 'timing', which means synchronising the subtitles to the dialogue and pictures.' This task requires discipline. 'You play the film, listen to the voice and the subtitles are up on your screen ready to be timed. You insert your subtitle when you hear the corresponding dialogue and delete it when the dialogue finishes. The video tape carries a time code which runs in hours, minutes, seconds and frames. Think of it as a clock. The subtitling unit has an insert key to capture the time code where you want the subtitle to appear. When you press the delete key, it captures the time code where you want the subtitle to disappear. So each subtitle would have an 'in' point and an 'out' point which represent

> **Subtitling is an exacting part of the translation profession. Melanie Leyshon talks to Virginie Verdier of London translation company VSI about the glamour and the grind**

the exact time when the subtitle comes in and goes out. This process is then followed by a manual review, subtitle by subtitle, and time-codes are adjusted to improve synchronisation and respect shot changes. This process involves playing the film literally frame by frame as it is essential the subtitles respect the visual rhythm of the film.'

Different subtitlers use different techniques. 'I would go through the film and do the whole translation and then go right back from the beginning and start the timing process. But you could do it in different stages, translate let's say 20 minutes of the film, then time this section and translate the next 20 minutes, and so on. It's just a different method.'

For multi-lingual projects, the timing is done first to create what is called a 'spotting list', a subtitle template, which is in effect a list of English subtitles pre-timed and edited for translation purposes. This is then translated and the timing is adapted to the target language with the help of the translator for quality control.

'Like any translation work, you can't hurry subtitling,' says Virginie. 'If subtitles are translated and timed in a rush, the quality will be affected and it will show.' Mistakes usually occur when the translator does not master the source language and misunderstands the original dialogue. 'Our work also involves checking and reworking subtitles when the translation is not up to standard. However, the reason for redoing subtitles is not just because of poor quality translation. We may need to adapt subtitles to a new version of the film: the time code may be different, the film may have been edited or the subtitles may have been created for the cinema rather than video. If subtitles were done for cinema on 35mm, we would need to reformat the timing for video, as subtitles could be out of synch or too fast. If the translation is good, we would obviously respect the work of the original translator.'

On a more practical level, there are general subtitling rules to follow, says Virginie. 'Subtitles should appear at the bottom of the screen and usually in the centre.' She says that different countries use different standards and rules. 'In Scandinavian countries and Holland, for example, subtitles are traditionally left justified. Characters usually appear in white with a thin black border for easy reading against a white or light background. We can also use different colours for each speaker when subtitling for the hearing impaired. Subtitles should have a maximum of two lines and the maximum number of characters on each line should be between 32 and 39. Our company standard is 37 (different companies and countries have different standards).'

Translators often have a favourite genre, whether it's war films, musicals, comedies (one of the most difficult because of the subtleties and nuances of comedy in different countries), drama or corporate programmes. Each requires a certain tone and style. 'VSI employs American subtitlers, which is incredibly useful as many of the films we subtitle are American,' says Virginie. 'For an English person, it would not be so easy to understand the meaning behind typically American expressions, and vice-versa.'

IELTS TEST 3

Exam Essentials

LISTENING MODULE   **READING MODULE**   WRITING MODULE   SPEAKING MODULE

PASSAGE 1
PASSAGE 2
PASSAGE 3

Questions 1–5

Complete the flow chart below.

Use **NO MORE THAN THREE WORDS** *from the passage for each answer.*

Write your answers in boxes 1–5 on your answer sheet.

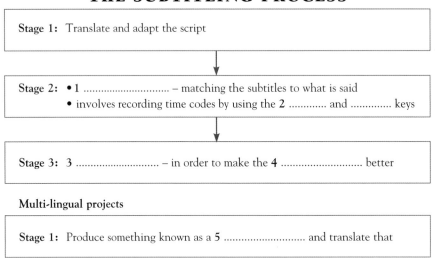

THE SUBTITLING PROCESS

Stage 1: Translate and adapt the script

Stage 2: • 1 .... – matching the subtitles to what is said
           • involves recording time codes by using the **2** .... and .... keys

Stage 3: **3** .... – in order to make the **4** .... better

Multi-lingual projects

Stage 1: Produce something known as a **5** .... and translate that

Questions 6–9

Do the following statements agree with the information given in Reading Passage 1?

In boxes 6–9 on your answer sheet write

    TRUE   *if the statement agrees with the information.*

    FALSE   *if the statement contradicts the information.*

    NOT GIVEN *if there is no information on this.*

6   For translators, all subtitling work on films is desirable.

7   Subtitling work involves a requirement that does not apply to other translation work.

8   Some subtitling techniques work better than others.

9   Few people are completely successful at subtitling comedies.

Questions 10–13

Complete the sentences below with words from Reading Passage 1.

Use **NO MORE THAN THREE WORDS** *for each answer.*

Write your answers in boxes 10–13 on your answer sheet.

10 Poor subtitling can be a result of the subtitler not being excellent at ....

11 To create subtitles for a video version of a film, it may be necessary to ....

12 Subtitles usually have a .... around them.

13 Speakers can be distinguished from each other for the benefit of ....

IELTS
TEST 3

Exam Essentials

LISTENING MODULE   READING MODULE   WRITING MODULE   SPEAKING MODULE

PASSAGE 1
PASSAGE 2
PASSAGE 3

You should spend about 20 minutes on **Questions 14–26**, *which are based on Reading Passage 2 on pages 100 and 101.*

Complementary and alternative medicine

WHAT DO SCIENTISTS IN BRITAIN THINK ABOUT 'ALTERNATIVE' THERAPIES? ORLA KENNEDY READS A SURPRISING SURVEY

Is complementary medicine hocus-pocus or does it warrant large-scale scientific investigation? Should science range beyond conventional medicine and conduct research on alternative medicine and the supposed growing links between mind and body? This will be hotly debated at the British Association for the Advancement of Science.

One Briton in five uses complementary medicine, and according to the most recent Mintel survey, one in ten uses herbalism or homoeopathy. Around £130 million is spent on oils, potions and pills every year in Britain, and the complementary and alternative medicine industry is estimated to be worth £1.6 billion. With the help of Professor Edzard Ernst, Laing, chair of complementary medicine at The Peninsula Medical School, Universities of Exeter and Plymouth, we asked scientists their views on complementary and alternative medicine. Seventy-five scientists, in fields ranging from molecular biology to neuroscience, replied.

Surprisingly, our sample of scientists was twice as likely as the public to use some form of complementary medicine, at around four in 10 compared with two in 10 of the general population. Three quarters of scientific users believed they were effective. Acupuncture, chiropractic and osteopathy were the most commonly used complementary treatments among scientists and more than 55 per cent believed these were more effective than a placebo and should be available to all on the National Health Service.

Scientists appear to place more trust in the more established areas of complementary and alternative medicine, such as acupuncture, chiropractic and osteopathy, for which there are professional bodies and recognised training, than therapies such as aroma therapy and spiritual healing. 'Osteopathy is now a registered profession requiring a certified four-year degree before you can advertise and practise,' said one neuroscientist who used the therapy.

Nearly two thirds of the scientists who replied to our survey believed that aromatherapy and homoeopathy were no better than placebos, with almost a half thinking the same of herbalism and spiritual thinking. Some of the comments we received were scathing, even though one in ten of our respondents had used homoeopathy. 'Aromatherapy and homoeopathy are scientifically nonsensical,' said one molecular biologist from the University of Bristol. Dr Romke Bron, a molecular biologist at the Medical Research Council Centre at King's College London, added: 'Homoeopathy is a big scam and I am convinced that if someone sneaked into a homoeopathic pharmacy and swapped labels, nobody would notice anything.'

Two centuries after homeopathy was introduced, it still lacks a watertight demonstration that it works. Scientists are happy that the resulting solutions and sugar pills have no side effects, but are baffled by how they can do anything.

Both complementary and conventional medicine should be used in routine health care, according to followers of the 'integrated health approach', who want to treat an individual 'as a whole'. But the scientists who responded to our survey expressed serious concerns about this approach, with more than half believing that integrated medicine was an attempt to bypass rigorous scientific testing. Dr Bron said: 'There is an awful lot of bad science going on in alternative medicine and the general public has a hard time to distinguish between scientific myth and fact. It is absolutely paramount to maintain rigorous quality control in health care. Although the majority of alternative health workers mean well, there are just too many frauds out there preying on vulnerable people.'

One molecular biologist from the University of Warwick admitted that 'by doing this poll I have realised how shamefully little I understand about alternative therapy. Not enough scientific research has been performed. There is enough anecdotal evidence to suggest that at least some of the alternative therapies are effective for some people, suggesting this is an area ripe for research.'

When asked if complementary and alternative medicine should get more research funding, scientists believed the top three (acupuncture, chiropractic and osteopathy) should get money, as should herbalism. It seems that therapies based on physical manipulation or a known action – like the active ingredients in a herb on a receptor in the body – are the ones that the scientific community has faith in. Less than a quarter thought that therapies such as aromatherapy, homoeopathy and spiritual healing should get any funding.

Scientists believed that the 'feelgood' counselling effect of complementary medicine and the time taken to listen to patients' problems was what worked, rather than any medicinal effect. In contrast, the average visit to the doctor lasts only eight minutes, says the British Medical Association. Dr Stephen Nurrish, a molecular biologist at University College London, said: 'Much of the benefit people get from complementary medicine is the time to talk to someone and be listened to sympathetically, something that is now lacking from medicine in general.'

But an anonymous neuroscientist at King's College London had a more withering view of this benefit: 'On the validity of complementary and alternative medicines, no one would dispute that 'feeling good' is good for your health, but why discriminate between museum-trip therapy, patting-a-dog therapy and aromatherapy? Is it because only the latter has a cadre of professional 'practitioners'?'

There are other hardline scientists who argue that there should be no such thing as complementary and alternative medicine. As Professor David Moore, director of the Medical Research Council's Institute for Hearing Research, said: 'Either a treatment works or it doesn't. The only way to determine if it works is to test it against appropriate controls (that is, scientifically).'

IELTS
TEST 3

Exam Essentials

LISTENING MODULE   READING MODULE   WRITING MODULE   SPEAKING MODULE

PASSAGE 1
PASSAGE 2
PASSAGE 3

Questions 14–19

*Look at the following views (**Questions 14–19**) and the list of people below them.*

Match each view with the person expressing it in the passage.

*Write the correct letter **A–E** in boxes 14–19 on your answer sheet.*

NB *You may use any letter more than once.*

14   Complementary medicine provides something that conventional medicine no longer does.

15   It is hard for people to know whether they are being told the truth or not.

16   Certain kinds of complementary and alternative medicine are taken seriously because of the number of people making money from them.

17   Nothing can be considered a form of medicine unless it has been proved effective.

18   It seems likely that some forms of alternative medicine do work.

19   One particular kind of alternative medicine is a deliberate attempt to cheat the public.

List of People

A   Dr Romke Bron
B   a molecular biologist from the University of Warwick
C   Dr Stephen Nurrish
D   a neuroscientist at King's College London
E   Professor David Moore

Questions 20–22

*Complete each sentence with the correct ending **A–F** from the box below.*

*Write the correct letter **A–F** in boxes 20–22 on your answer sheet.*

20   The British Association for the Advancement of Science will be discussing the issue of

21   A recent survey conducted by a certain organisation addressed the issue of

22   The survey in which the writer of the article was involved gave information on

---

A   what makes people use complementary rather than conventional medicine.
B   how many scientists themselves use complementary and alternative medicine.
C   whether alternative medicine should be investigated scientifically.
D   research into the use of complementary and conventional medicine together.
E   how many people use various kinds of complementary medicine.
F   the extent to which attitudes to alternative medicine are changing.

Questions 23–26

Classify the following information as being given about

A	acupuncture
B	aromatherapy
C	herbalism
D	homoeopathy

Write the correct letter, **A**, **B**, **C** *or* **D** *in boxes 23–26 on your answer sheet.*

23 Scientists believe that it is ineffective but harmless.

24 Scientists felt that it could be added to the group of therapies that deserved to be provided with resources for further investigation.

25 Scientists felt that it deserved to be taken seriously because of the organised way in which it has developed.

26 A number of scientists had used it, but harsh criticism was expressed about it.

IELTS
TEST 3

Exam Essentials

LISTENING MODULE   READING MODULE   WRITING MODULE   SPEAKING MODULE

PASSAGE 1
PASSAGE 2
PASSAGE 3

▸ **Questions 27–40**

You should spend about 20 minutes on **Questions 27–40**, *which are based on Reading Passage 3 on pages 105–106.*

Questions 27–32

Reading Passage 3 has six paragraphs **A–F**.

Choose the correct heading for each paragraph from the list of headings below.

Write the correct number **i–x** *in boxes 27–32 on your answer sheet.*

List of Headings
i   A surprising discovery
ii   Unlikely consequences
iii   A safe route
iv   A controversial system
v   An ill-chosen departure
vi   An enlarged breeding place
vii   Arguing against critics
viii   An all-too-frequent tragedy
ix   A previous vision
x   Accommodating all

27   Paragraph **A**

28   Paragraph **B**

29   Paragraph **C**

30   Paragraph **D**

31   Paragraph **E**

32   Paragraph **F**

PATH OF THE JAGUAR

A At dusk one evening, deep in a Costa Rican forest, a young male jaguar rises from his sleep, stretches, and silently but determinedly leaves forever the place where he was born. But the wanderer has chosen the wrong direction. In just a few miles he reaches the edge of the forest; beyond lies a coffee plantation. Pushed by instinct and necessity, he keeps moving, staying in the trees along fences and streams. Soon, though, shelter consists only of scattered patches of shrubs and a few trees, where he can find nothing to eat. He's now in a land of cattle ranches, and one night his hunger and the smell of a new-born calf overcome his reluctance to cross open areas. Creeping close before a final rush, he instantly kills the calf with one snap of his powerful jaws.

B The next day the rancher finds the remains and the tell-tale tracks of a jaguar. He calls some of his neighbours and gathers a pack of dogs. The hunters find the young male, but they're armed only with shotguns; anxious, they shoot from too great a distance. The jaguar's massively thick skull protects him from death, but the pellets blind him in one eye and shatter his left foreleg. Unable to find his normal prey in the scrubby forest, he kills another calf on an adjacent ranch, and then a dog on the outskirts of a nearby town. This time, though, he lingers too long. Attracted by the dog's howls, a group of villagers find him and, though it takes many blasts, kill him. This sad story has been played out thousands of times throughout the jaguar's homeland, as ranching, farming and development have eaten up half the big cat's prime habitat, and as humans have decimated its natural prey in many areas of remaining forest.

C Alan Rabinowitz envisions a different ending to the story. He imagines that the young jaguar, when he leaves his birthplace, will pass unseen by humans through a near-continuous corridor of sheltering vegetation. Within a couple of days he'll find a small tract of forest harbouring enough prey for him to stop and rest a day or two before resuming his trek. Studies have shown that areas smaller than four square kilometres can serve as temporary, one- or two-day homes—stepping-stones—for wandering jaguars. Eventually he'll reach a national park or wildlife preserve where he'll find a home, plenty of prey, and females looking for a mate. Rabinowitz is the world's leading jaguar expert, and he has begun to realise his dream of creating a vast network of interconnected corridors and refuges extending from the U.S.-Mexico border into South America. It is known as Paseo del Jaguar—Path of the Jaguar. Rabinowitz considers such a network the best hope for keeping this great New World cat from joining lions and tigers on the endangered species list.

D Rabinowitz began his work with the Wildlife Conservation Society and now heads the Panthera Foundation, a conservation group

IELTS TEST 3

Exam Essentials

LISTENING MODULE   READING MODULE   WRITING MODULE   SPEAKING MODULE

PASSAGE 1
PASSAGE 2
PASSAGE 3

dedicated to protecting the world's 36 species of wild cats. The foundation's current work represents a radical change in Rabinowitz's conservation philosophy from just a decade ago. In the 1990s, having censused jaguars across their range, Rabinowitz and other specialists identified dozens of what they called jaguar conservation units (JCUs): large areas with perhaps 50 jaguars, where the local population was either stable or increasing. At the heart of most of the JCUs were existing parks or other protected areas, which Rabinowitz hoped to expand and secure with surrounding buffer zones.

E Within a few years, though, the new science of DNA fingerprinting—studying genetic material to determine family and species relationships—revealed an amazing fact: The jaguar is the only large, wide-ranging carnivore in the world with no subspecies. Simply put, this means that for millennia jaguars have been mingling their genes throughout their entire range, so that individuals in northern Mexico are identical to those in southern Brazil. For that to be true, some of the cats must wander regularly and widely between populations. Rabinowitz and his colleagues went back to their data to see whether the preserves could still be linked with habitat adequate to support a traveling jaguar. "Lo and behold," Rabinowitz said, "while good jaguar habitat, where the cats can live and breed, has decreased by 50 percent since the 1900s, habitat a jaguar can use to travel through has decreased only by 16 percent. Most of it is intact and contiguous. These places are like little oases—very small patches that jaguars will come to, use a while, and then leave. We were writing these places off because they're not habitat where a permanent jaguar population can live. Now they're turning out to be crucial."

F Rabinowitz hopes to convince national governments throughout the jaguar's range to maintain this web of habitat through enlightened land-use planning, such as choosing noncritical areas for major developments and road construction. "We're not going to ask them to throw people off their land or to make new national parks," he said. The habitat matrix could encompass woodlands used for a variety of human activities from timber harvest to citrus plantations.

Questions 33–36

Label the diagram below.

Choose **NO MORE THAN THREE WORDS AND/OR A NUMBER** *from the passage for each answer.*

Write your answers in boxes 33–36 on your answer sheet.

Path of the Jaguar

33 Passageway of ....
trees and plants

34 Temporary resting place for
duration of up to ....

35 Needs to be only as
big as ....

Route

Route

36 Wildlife park area containing
sufficient .... and
mating partners

Questions 37–40

Reading Passage 3 has six paragraphs labelled **A–F**.

Which paragraph contains the following information?

Write the correct letter **A–F** *in boxes 37–40 on your answer sheet.*

NB *You may use any letter more than once.*

37 a realisation of the importance of something that had been overlooked

38 an example of the consequences for a jaguar of delaying departure

39 a reference to the fact that certain areas had mistakenly been ruled out as jaguar homes

40 details of a strategy that was later abandoned

IELTS
TEST 3

Exam Essentials

LISTENING MODULE   READING MODULE   **WRITING MODULE**   SPEAKING MODULE

Task 1
Task 2

You should spend about 20 minutes on this task.

The graphs below show the number of drivers in Britain who have been caught driving too fast by speed cameras placed on roads, and the number of people killed in road accidents, over an eight-year period since the introduction of speed cameras. The tables show the results of a survey on people's opinions on speed cameras.

Summarise the information by selecting and reporting the main features and make comparisons where relevant.

Write at least 150 words.

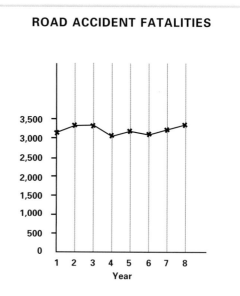

Do you think speed cameras reduce the number of accidents on the roads?

Yes	32%
No	60%
Don't know	8%

What do you think is the main reason for the installation of speed cameras?

To improve road safety	26%
To raise revenue	71%
Don't know	3%

What do you think about the number of speed cameras on the roads?

Too many	56%
Too few	19%
About right	17%
Don't know	8%

There is a sample answer on page 201.

You should spend about 40 minutes on this task.

Present a written argument or case to an educated reader with no specialist knowledge of the following topic.

> *In some countries today, there is an attitude that 'anyone can do it' in the arts – music, literature, acting, art, etc. As a result, people with no talent become rich and famous and genuine talent is not valued or appreciated.*
>
> *Do you agree or disagree?*

You should use your own ideas, knowledge and experience and support your arguments with examples and relevant evidence.

Write at least 250 words.

There is a sample answer on page 201.

▸ PART 1

Example questions

- What subject did you find most interesting when you were at school?
- Apart from classes, what else did you enjoy at school?
- Do you think that you will stay friends with people from your school?
- What study or training would you like to do in the future?

▸ PART 2

Example task

Read the topic card below carefully.

You will have to talk about the topic for one to two minutes.

You have one minute to think about what you're going to say.

You can make notes to help you if you wish.

> **Describe a holiday you would like to go on.**
> **You should say:**
>
> - what place you would like to go to
> - how you would like to get there
> - what you would like to do while you were there
>
> and explain why you would like to go on this holiday.

▸ PART 3

Example questions

- Which places in your country do you think visitors would enjoy visiting most?
- What are the benefits of going away on holiday?
- What kinds of benefits might a significant increase in tourist numbers bring to a location?
- What developments affecting international travel might there be in the future?

IELTS TEST 4

Exam Essentials

| LISTENING MODULE | READING MODULE | WRITING MODULE | SPEAKING MODULE |

SECTION 1
SECTION 2
SECTION 3
SECTION 4

▶ **Questions 1–10**

Complete the form below.

Write **NO MORE THAN THREE WORDS AND/OR A NUMBER** *for each answer.*

ABLE EMPLOYMENT AGENCY

APPLICATION FORM

Full name: 1...
Address: 2...
               Melford MF4 5JB

Contact number: 3...

Qualifications: (a) A levels
                (b) **4** ....
                (c) **5**..

Previous experience: (a) general work in a **6** .... (3 months)
                (b) part-time job as a **7** ....

Interests: (a) member of a **8** ....
                (b) enjoys **9** .... (10 years)

Date available: **10** ....

LISTENING MODULE	READING MODULE	WRITING MODULE	SPEAKING MODULE

SECTION 1
SECTION 2
SECTION 3
SECTION 4

▶ **Questions 11–20**

Questions 11–16

Complete the sentences below.

Write **NO MORE THAN TWO WORDS** *for each answer.*

The hotel

11 You must book .... in advance.

12 There are some interesting .... in the lounge.

Activities

13 The visit to the .... has been cancelled.

14 There will be a talk about .... from the area on Saturday.

15 The visit to the .... will take place on Sunday.

16 There is a collection of .... in the art gallery.

Questions 17–20

Label the map below.

Write the correct letter **A–I** *next to questions 17–20.*

Where are the following places situated?

17 Park Hotel   ....

18 Internet Café   ....

19 Tourist Information Office   ....

20 Royal House Restaurant   ....

▶ **Questions 21–30**

Questions 21–26

*Write the correct letter, **A**, **B** or **C** next to questions 21–26.*

At which college are the following features recommended?

A at Forth College
B at Haines College
C at both Forth and Haines Colleges

21 student support services
22 residential accommodation
23 on-line resources
24 libraries
25 teaching staff
26 research record

Questions 27–30

*Choose the correct letter, **A**, **B** or **C**.*

27 David is concerned that he may feel
   A unmotivated.
   B isolated.
   C competitive.

28 In the future, Dr Smith thinks David should aim to
   A do further research.
   B publish articles.
   C get teaching work.

29 What does Dr Smith think has improved masters' study in recent years?
   A the development of the internet
   B the growth of flexible courses
   C the introduction of changes in assessment

30 David would like to improve the way he
   A takes notes in lectures.
   B writes up assignments.
   C manages his time.

| LISTENING MODULE | READING MODULE | WRITING MODULE | SPEAKING MODULE |

SECTION 1
SECTION 2
SECTION 3
SECTION 4

▶ **Questions 31–40**

Questions 31–37

Complete the table below.

Write **NO MORE THAN TWO WORDS** *for each answer.*

Type of writing	Notes	Tips
Short stories	3 basic styles	start with a 31 ....
Non-fiction	biographies often popular	tell publishers about your 32 ....
Articles	advice articles work well	write for a 33 ....
Poetry	meaning shouldn't be too 34	read your poems aloud
Plays	movements usually decided by the 35	learn about acting
Radio	BBC publishes Handbook	try 36 .... first
Children's literature	illustrations important	decide on an 37 ....

Questions 38–40

Choose the correct letter, **A**, **B** *or* **C**.

38 What is a disadvantage of first person narration in novels?
   A It makes it harder for the main character to be interesting.
   B It is difficult for beginners to do well.
   C It limits what can be described.

39 What is a mistake when writing novels?
   A failing to include enough detail
   B trying to explain ironic effects
   C including too many characters

40 In order to make dialogue seem natural, writers should
   A make recordings of real conversations.
   B include unfinished sentences.
   C break up long speeches.

IELTS TEST 4

Exam Essentials

LISTENING MODULE   **READING MODULE**   WRITING MODULE   SPEAKING MODULE

PASSAGE 1
PASSAGE 2
PASSAGE 3

You should spend about 20 minutes on **Questions 1–13**, *which are based on Reading Passage 1 on pages 116 and 117.*

Groucho Marx & Arthur Sheekman

In a show-business career that spanned over seventy years, Groucho Marx successfully conquered every entertainment medium, becoming a star of the vaudeville stage, Broadway, motion pictures, radio and television. But, as the author of seven books, a play, two film screenplays and over one hundred magazine articles and essays, Groucho quietly conquered another medium, one in which he was as proud to work as any of the others. His writing is often overlooked in studies of his career, perhaps due to the quantity and variety of his other work.

Throughout his literary career, Groucho was dogged by the incorrect and unfair assumption by many critics and even by his biographer that he used a ghost writer. Most Hollywood celebrities who wrote books had professional writers do the actual work. The fact that Groucho publicly stated on many occasions that he abhorred ghost writers is clouded by his relationship with Arthur Sheekman. Friends for many years, Groucho and Sheekman had an unusual literary relationship. They worked in collaboration and each offered the other editorial help. For a brief time in the early 1940s, Groucho fronted for Sheekman, who was having trouble selling his work. By thus lending his name to another writer's work, Groucho subjected all of his literary endeavors to suspicion from critics who simply refused to believe that an entertainer could write.

That some of Sheekman's magazine pieces got into print under Groucho's byline becomes apparent from reading the unedited correspondence between the two of them. The letters indicate that Groucho's essays from this period fall into three categories: first, pieces written by Groucho with no input from Sheekman at all. In a July 1, 1940, letter to Sheekman, Groucho asked, 'Did you see that little piece I wrote for *Reader's Digest?*' On March 17, 1941, he wrote, 'My drool is coming out in next week's issue of *This Week* so cancel your subscription now.' Clearly Sheekman could not have had anything to do with a piece that he was told to look for.

The second and probably largest category of Groucho's essays of this period consists of those written by Groucho and sent to Sheekman for editorial assistance. On July 20, 1940, Groucho wrote: 'I'm enclosing a copy of the piece I wrote. Probably another page or so is needed to complete it, but our starting date [for filming *Go West*] came and I just haven't had time to finish it. Let me know what you think of it and be honest because any other kind of opinion would be of no value to me. I won't attempt to influence you by telling you the reactions I've already had, so for the love of God tell me the truth.' Shortly thereafter, on October 10, Groucho wrote: 'I received your suggestions on my piece – I'm glad you liked it, if you did – you're probably right about the beginning. I'll do it over again.' By the time Groucho wrote to Sheekman on July 25, 1942, it appears that some sort of financial arrangement had been made regarding Sheekman's suggestions. On that date Groucho also wrote: 'I'm writing an unfunny piece on insomnia and I'll send it in a week or so, I hope, for you to read – I'd like your opinion, proofread – correcting all the glaring illiteracies and, otherwise, do a fine polishing job.'

The remainder of Groucho's essays from this period comprise the third category, Sheekman compositions with varying degrees of input from Groucho. The level of Groucho's contributions to the articles in the third category ranges from actually suggesting the topic and drawing up an outline to simply rewriting a few paragraphs for the purpose of injecting his own style into the piece. In a July 10, 1940, letter Groucho wrote: 'I think you ought to try another political piece – a campaign thing – for *This Week* or some other magazine. This will be an extremely hot topic for the next few months and I think you should take advantage of it. If you'll write to me, I'll try to jot down a few items that you could complain about.' Presumably, the chain of events would continue with Sheekman sending an essay to Groucho for his approval and whatever rewrites were needed. On May 29, 1940, Groucho wrote, 'Received your piece and looked it over.' In these letters to Sheekman, Groucho always referred to a piece as either 'my piece' or 'your piece'. The letter continued, 'I thought the piece was good ... and I'll send it to Bye and see if he can sell it ... I'll just rewrite a couple of paragraphs in your piece – not that I can improve them, but perhaps they'll sound a little more like me.' Groucho was concerned enough about this arrangement to take the care to at least make the piece somewhat his own.

Groucho really had no need for this entire enterprise. He gave the money to Sheekman and had no trouble getting his own work published. The principal reason for him submitting Sheekman's work to magazines as his own was that it made Sheekman's material easily marketable based on Groucho's celebrity. Sheekman couldn't have been altogether happy with the arrangement, but the reality was that he was periodically unemployed and the use of Groucho's name brought in occasional paychecks. So it is not quite fair to call Sheekman Groucho's ghost writer. A more apt description of their literary relationship at this time is that Groucho occasionally fronted for Sheekman and offered him the services of his literary agent, while each offered the other editorial advice. The reasons for some of their collaborative efforts not being credited as such remain unexplained, but Groucho was never shy about crediting his collaborators, and in every other case he did so.

IELTS TEST 4

Exam Essentials

LISTENING MODULE   READING MODULE   WRITING MODULE   SPEAKING MODULE

PASSAGE 1
PASSAGE 2
PASSAGE 3

Questions 1–4

Do the following statements reflect the claims of the writer of Reading Passage 1?

In boxes 1–4 on your answer sheet write

YES	*if the statement agrees with the claims of the writer.*
NO	*if the statement contradicts the claims of the writer.*
NOT GIVEN	*if it is impossible to say what the writer thinks about this.*

1 Groucho's work as a writer was sometimes better than his work in other media.
2 Groucho's relationship with Sheekman cast doubt on his own abilities as a writer.
3 Money was occasionally a source of disagreement between Groucho and Sheekman.
4 Groucho occasionally regretted his involvement with Sheekman.

Questions 5–8

Complete the notes below.

*Choose **NO MORE THAN THREE WORDS** from the passage for each answer.*

Write your answers in boxes 5–8 on your answer sheet.

Groucho's essays in the early 1940s

Category 1	Category 2	Category 3
Sheekman had 5	Sheekman provided 6	mostly 7 .... Groucho added 8 ....

Questions 9–13

Look at the following statements (Questions 9–13) and the list of dates of letters sent by Groucho to Sheekman below.

Match each statement with the letter it relates to.

*Write the correct letter **A–G** in boxes 9–13 on your answer sheet.*

9 Groucho referred to his own inadequacy with regard to use of language.

10 Groucho explained his reason for amending an essay.

11 Groucho agreed that part of an essay needed revising.

12 Groucho drew Sheekman's attention to an essay soon to be published.

13 Groucho suggested that an essay should adopt a negative point of view.

List of Letters Sent by Groucho to Sheekman	
A	July 1, 1940
B	March 17, 1941
C	July 20, 1940
D	October 10, 1940
E	July 25, 1942
F	July 10, 1940
G	May 29, 1940

You should spend about 20 minutes on **Questions 14–26**, *which are based on Reading Passage 2 on pages 120 and 121.*

An earth-shaking discovery

The discovery of sea floor spreading is earth-shaking, yet those responsible are forgotten, says Anna Grayson

In 1963, a paper appeared in the journal *Nature* that radically changed the way we view this planet and its resources. Its authors, Fred Vine and Drummond Matthews, did for the Earth sciences what Crick and Watson did for biology and Einstein did for physics, and new areas of scientific development are still emerging as a result.

Yet both men are largely forgotten and unrecognised. What Vine and Matthews did was to provide proof that continents really do drift across the surface of the globe. This understanding profoundly affects the way we use the planet today – it directs the way we prospect for resources such as oil and minerals; it has enabled us to predict most volcanic eruptions and to understand patterns of earthquakes. Incredibly, perhaps, an understanding of the mobile dynamic nature of the Earth is helping an understanding of long-term global climate changes. Despite the significance of their work, neither man received great honour or fame.

The idea of continental drift was first proposed in a serious way by the German meteorologist Alfred Wegener in 1915. People had noticed the neat jigsaw-like fit between South America and Africa, but Wegener found actual fossil evidence that the two continents were once joined. No one took him seriously; in fact he was ridiculed by most of the geological community. This was partly because, not being a geologist, he was perceived as an outsider. But the main reason for the hostility, according to Vine, was that Wegener was unable to come up with an explanation as to how whole continents could possibly move even an inch, let alone dance to the music of time around the globe.

In the 1920s, the Scottish geologist Arthur Holmes hypothesised that convection currents within the Earth 'could become sufficiently vigorous to drag the two halves of the original continent apart'. In the late 1950s, an American, Harry Hess, came up with the hypothesis that new sea floor is constantly being generated at the mid-ocean ridges by hot material rising in a convection current. But neither man could find evidence to prove it. It was no more than just a hunch that it had to be right, and a hunch is not enough for science.

Vine had been fascinated by the apparent fit of the continents since the age of 14, and as a graduate student at Cambridge was assigned a project analysing one of the new magnetic surveys of the ocean floor. He found what he describes as 'parallel zebra stripes of normal and reversed magnetism' around the mid-ocean ridge. Most significantly, these stripes were symmetrical either side of the ridge crests. There had to be a reason for this. The young Vine and his supervisor Matthews proposed that the magnetic stripes were caused by new ocean floor being formed as molten rock rose at the mid-ocean ridges and spread each side of the ridge.

As the molten rock solidified, it became weakly magnetised parallel to the Earth's magnetic field. It was just becoming recognised in the early 1960s that the Earth's magnetic field flips every so often, so magnetic north becomes a magnetic south pole and visa versa. These flips in magnetic field were being recorded in the new sea floor. It was like a giant tape recording of the ocean floor's history. As new sea floor was made, it pushed the last lot aside, widening the ocean and in turn pushing the continents either side further apart. In other words, they had discovered the mechanism driving drifting continents that was missing from Wegener's work. The science of the Earth was never the same again.

By the end of the 1960s, confirmation of global sea floor spreading led to plate tectonics – the view of the outside of the Earth comprising just a few rigid plates which are shunted about by growing sea floor. There was a realisation that mountains are formed when two plates collide, and that most volcanoes and earthquakes occur on the edges of these plates. All this was accepted as fact by all but a few die-hard dinosaurs in the geological world.

It is now in the impact of shifting continents on the global environment that Vine feels the most exciting and significant research lies: 'The distribution of continents and the opening and closing of ocean gates between continents has had a profound effect on climates and has caused flips from Ice-house Earth to Green-house Earth.'

The recognition that the Earth's hydrosphere, atmosphere and biosphere are all intimately linked with the drifting continents and the goings-on deep within the Earth has spawned the term 'Earth Systems Science'. It is a great oak tree of science that has grown from the acorn of truth supplied by Vine and Matthews. The holistic approach of earth systems science is very much welcomed by Vine: 'I'm rather pleased that this has come together.' He feels that the future for understanding the planet lies in an integrated approach to the sciences, rather than the isolated stance the geologists took throughout the 20th century: 'There was an incredible polarisation of science and I was caught between the boundaries. It was anathema to me – the whole of environmental science should be integrated.'

PASSAGE 1
PASSAGE 2
PASSAGE 3

Questions 14–17

Complete each sentence with the correct ending **A–G** *from the box below.*

Write the correct letter **A–G** *in boxes 14–17 on your answer sheet.*

14 The work done by Vine and Matthews has had implications concerning

15 Wegener attempted to provide an explanation of

16 Wegener's conclusions were greeted as

17 The theories presented by both Holmes and Hess concerned

A matters that had not received much attention for some time.
B something which could not possibly be true.
C something misunderstood at first but later seen as a breakthrough.
D matters beyond simply the movement of continents.
E something that had already been observed.
F something arrived at by intuition that could not be demonstrated.
G matters requiring different research techniques.

Questions 18–22

Label the diagram below.

Choose **NO MORE THAN THREE WORDS** *from the passage for each answer.*

Write your answers in boxes 18–22 on your answer sheet.

THE DISCOVERIES OF VINE AND MATTHEWS

The Ocean Floor

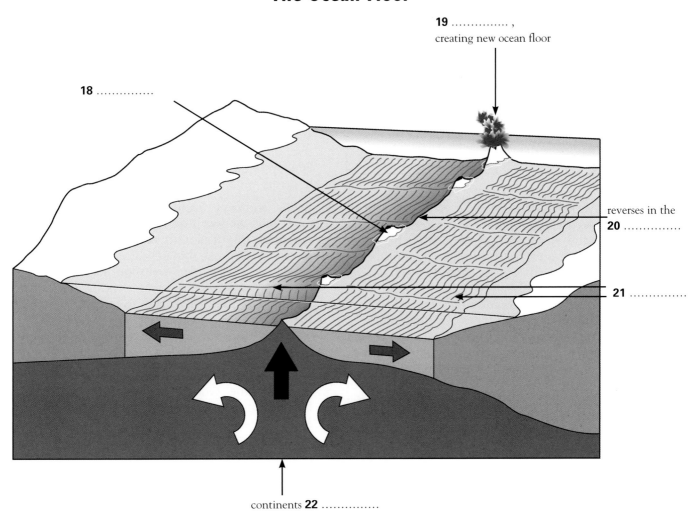

19 .... ,
creating new ocean floor

18 ....

reverses in the
20 ....

21 ....

continents **22** ....

Questions 23–26

Answer the questions below using **NO MORE THAN THREE WORDS** *for each answer.*

Write your answers in boxes 23–26 on your answer sheet.

23 What is the name of the theory concerning the structure of the Earth that developed from the demonstration of sea floor spreading?

24 According to Vine, what has the movement of continents had a big influence on?

25 What branch of science has emerged as a result of the work done by Vine and Matthews?

26 Which word does Vine use to describe the way in which he believes study of the Earth should be conducted?

You should spend about 20 minutes on **Questions 27–40**, *which are based on Reading Passage 3 on pages 124 and 125.*

Think happy

It's no joke: even scientists at the Royal Society are now taking the search for the source of happiness very seriously

A What would Sir Isaac Newton have made of it? There he was, painted in oils, gazing down at one of the strangest meetings that the Royal Society, Britain's most august scientific body, has ever held. If Newton had flashed a huge grin, it would have been completely appropriate, for beneath him last week a two-day conference was unfolding on a booming new field of science: investigating what makes people happy. Distinguished professors strode up to the podium, including one eminent neurologist armed with videos of women giggling at comedy films; another was a social scientist brandishing statistics on national cheerfulness. Hundreds of other researchers sat scribbling notes on how to produce more smiles.

B The decision by the Royal Society to pick 'the science of wellbeing' from hundreds of applications for conferences on other topics is no laughing matter. It means that the investigation of what makes people happy is being taken very seriously indeed. 'Many philosophies and religions have studied this subject, but scientifically it has been ignored,' said Dr Nick Baylis, a Cambridge University psychologist and one of the conference organisers. 'For the Royal Society to give us its countenance is vital, because that states that what we are doing deserves to be acknowledged and investigated by the best scientific minds.'

C At first sight, the mission of Baylis – and the growing number of other scientists working on happiness research – appears fanciful. They want to deploy scientifically rigorous methods to determine why some people are lastingly happy while others tend to misery. Then they envisage spreading the secret of happiness across the globe and, in short, increasing the sum of human happiness. 'If someone is happy, they are more popular and also healthier, they live longer and are more productive at work. So it is very much worth having,' he says.

D Baylis, the only 'positive psychology' lecturer in Britain, knows that the aims of happiness research might sound woolly, so he is at pains to distance himself from the brigades of non-academic self-help gurus. He refers to 'life satisfaction' and 'wellbeing' and emphasises that his work, and that of others at the conference, is grounded in solid research. So what have the scientists discovered – has a theory of happiness been defined yet?

E According to Professor Martin Seligman, probably the world's leading figure in this field, happiness could be but a train ride – and a couple of questionnaires – away. It was Seligman, a psychologist from Pennsylvania University, who kick-started the happiness science movement with a speech he made as President of the American Psychological Association (APA). Why, asked Seligman, shocking delegates at an APA conference, does science only investigate suffering? Why not look into what steps increase happiness, even for those who are not depressed, rather than simply seek to assuage pain? For a less well-known scientist, the speech could have spelt the end of a career, but instead Seligman landed funding of almost £18m to follow his hunch. He has been in regular contact with hundreds of other researchers and practising psychologists around the world, all the while conducting polls and devising strategies for increasing happiness.

F His findings have led him to believe that there are three main types of happiness. First, there is 'the pleasant life' – the kind of happiness we usually gain from sensual pleasures such as eating and drinking or watching a good film. Seligman blames Hollywood and the advertising industry for encouraging the rest of us, wrongly as he sees it, to believe that lasting happiness is to be found that way. Second, there is 'the good life', which comes from enjoying something we are good or talented at. The key to this, Seligman believes, lies in identifying our strengths and then taking part in an activity that uses them. Third, there is 'the meaningful life'. The most lasting happiness, Seligman says, comes from finding something you believe in and then putting your strengths at its service. People who are good at communicating with others might thus find long-lasting happiness through becoming involved in politics or voluntary work, while a rock star wanting to save the world might find it in organising a charity concert.

G Achieving 'the good life' and 'the meaningful life' is the secret of lasting happiness, Seligman says. For anybody unsure of how to proceed, he has an intriguing idea. To embark on the road to happiness, he suggests that you need a pen, some paper and, depending on your location, a railway ticket. First, identify a person to whom you feel a deep debt of gratitude but have never thanked properly. Next, write a 300-word essay outlining how important the help was and how much you appreciate it. Then tell them you need to visit, without saying what for, turn up at their house and read them the essay. The result: tears, hugs and deeper, longer-lasting happiness, apparently, than would come from any amount of champagne.

H Sceptics may insist that science will always remain a clumsy way of investigating and propagating happiness and say that such things are better handled by artists, writers and musicians – if they can be handled at all. And not everybody at the conference was positive about the emerging science. Lewis Wolpert, professor of biology as applied to medicine at University College London, who has written a bestseller about his battle with depression, said: 'If you were really totally happy, I'd be very suspicious. I think you wouldn't do anything, you'd just sort of sit there in a treacle of happiness. There's a whole world out there, and unless you have a bit of discomfort, you'll never actually do anything.'

IELTS
TEST 4

Exam Essentials

LISTENING MODULE   READING MODULE   WRITING MODULE   SPEAKING MODULE

PASSAGE 1
PASSAGE 2
PASSAGE 3

Questions 27–30

Complete the sentences below with words taken from Reading Passage 3.

Use **NO MORE THAN THREE WORDS** *for each answer.*

Write your answers in boxes 27–30 on your answer sheet.

27   At the conference, research into happiness was referred to as the ....

28   Baylis and others intend to use .... to find out what makes people happy or unhappy.

29   Baylis gives classes on the subject of ....

30   Baylis says he should not be categorised among the .... who do not have academic credentials.

Questions 31–36

Complete the summary below using words from the box.

Write your answers in boxes 31–36 on your answer sheet.

Seligman's categories of happiness

Seligman's first type of happiness involves the enjoyment of pleasures such as **31** .... He believes that people should not be under the **32** .... that such things lead to happiness that is not just temporary. His second type is related to **33** .... Identification of this should lead to **34** .... and the result is 'the good life'. His third type involves having a strong **35** .... and doing something about it for the benefit of others. This, according to Seligman, leads to happiness that has some **36** ....

confidence	entertainment	incentive	leadership
thrill	perseverance	illusion	effort
ability	theory	celebration	participation
ego	permanence	leadership	encouragement
exaggeration	concept	conviction	support

Questions 37–40

Reading Passage 3 has eight paragraphs labelled **A–H**.

Which paragraph contains the following information?

Write the correct letter **A–H** *in boxes 37–40 on your answer sheet.*

37   a view that complete happiness may not be a desirable goal

38   a reference to the potential wider outcomes of conducting research into happiness

39   an implication of the fact that the conference was held at all

40   a statement concerning the possible outcome of expressing a certain view in public

You should spend about 20 minutes on this task.

> *The diagram below shows the process for making a water clock.*
>
> *Summarise the information by selecting and reporting the main features, and make comparisons where relevant.*

Write at least 150 words.

HOW TO BUILD YOUR OWN WATER CLOCK

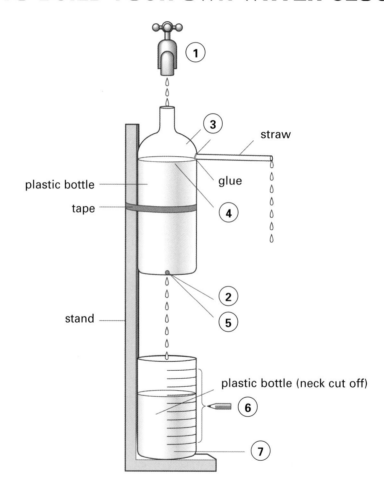

STAGES

1   tap on
2   cover hole with finger
3   fill top bottle to overflow
4   level constant
5   finger away from hole
6   levels per minute
7   empty and repeat process for timing things

There is a task guide for this task type on page 230 and a sample answer on page 202.

You should spend about 40 minutes on this task.

Present a written argument or case to an educated reader with no specialist knowledge of the following topic.

> *In some countries, it can be very difficult for people over the age of 50 to get good jobs, despite their experience.*
>
> *What do you think are the causes of this problem, and what measures could be taken to solve it?*

You should use your own ideas, knowledge and experience and support your arguments with examples and relevant evidence.

Write at least 250 words.

There is a sample answer on page 202.

▸ PART 1

Example questions

- What sorts of food do you enjoy eating most?
- Do you spend much time shopping for food?
- Which do you prefer, eating at home or eating in restaurants?
- Do you think people should be careful about what they eat?

▸ PART 2

Example task

Read the topic card below carefully.

You will have to talk about the topic for one to two minutes.

You have one minute to think about what you are going to say.

You can make notes if you want.

> **Describe a town you have enjoyed visiting.**
>
> **You should say:**
>
> - **why you went to the town**
>
> - **who you saw there**
>
> - **what you did there**
>
> **and explain why you enjoyed visiting the town.**

▸ PART 3

Example questions

- What are the kinds of things people like to do when visiting towns and cities?
- Why do many people prefer to live in cities rather than in the countryside?
- Can you identify some of the main problems of living in large cities?
- What measures could be taken to reduce problems of congestion in cities?

IELTS
TEST 5

Exam Essentials

| LISTENING MODULE | READING MODULE | WRITING MODULE | SPEAKING MODULE |

SECTION 1
SECTION 2
SECTION 3
SECTION 4

▶ **Questions 1–10**

Questions 1–6

Write **NO MORE THAN TWO WORDS AND/OR A NUMBER** *for each answer.*

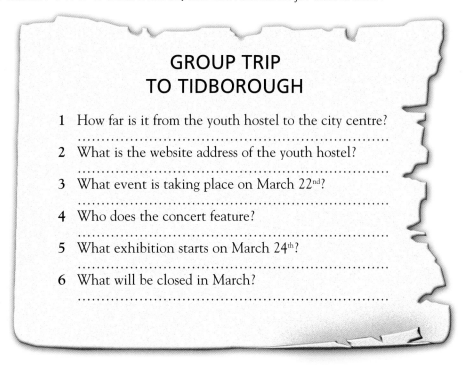

GROUP TRIP
TO TIDBOROUGH

1 How far is it from the youth hostel to the city centre?
....

2 What is the website address of the youth hostel?
....

3 What event is taking place on March 22nd?
....

4 Who does the concert feature?
....

5 What exhibition starts on March 24th?
....

6 What will be closed in March?
....

Questions 7–10

Choose the correct letters **A–C**.

7 When does the train ride depart?
  A 9.00
  B 9.15
  C 9.30

8 Where is it recommended to buy tickets?
  A at the tourist office
  B at the station
  C at the youth hostel

9 How much is the group discount?
  A 10%
  B 15%
  C 20%

10 How long does the excursion last?
  A 3 hours
  B 3½ hours
  C 4 hours

▶ *Questions 11–20*

Questions 11–13

Choose the correct letter, A, B or C.

11   Which chart shows the company's sales figures for the last five years?

12   Which chart shows the relationship of three departments this year?

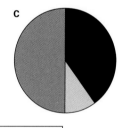

Food   Clothing   Electrical

13   Which chart shows numbers of temporary staff in the company?

Questions 14–19

Complete the notes below.

Write **NO MORE THAN TWO WORDS** *for each answer.*

- Company's mission statement: '**14** ……………..…………………… for customers'

- In case of problems, always ask your **15** …………………………………… for help

- Important for customers to have a **16** …………………………………… experience

- Tell customers about **17** ………………………………… goods

- Read the **18** ………………………………… every month

- Must attend **19** ………………………………… on Thursdays

Question 20

Choose **TWO** *letters* **A–E**.

20 Which **TWO** things must be done today?
- **A** complete form
- **B** get security pass
- **C** register for discount
- **D** show certificates
- **E** watch information video

IELTS TEST 5

Exam Essentials

| LISTENING MODULE | READING MODULE | WRITING MODULE | SPEAKING MODULE |

SECTION 1
SECTION 2
SECTION 3
SECTION 4

▸ **Questions 21–30**

Questions 21–24

Which action does each type of penguin do?

Choose your answers **A–G** *from the box below and write them next to questions 21–24.*

A	always hesitate before jumping
B	avoid climbing if possible
C	lean backwards when calling
D	move around at night
E	use its bill when climbing
F	usually look twice at things
G	walk with its flippers pointing downwards

21 Gentoo ....

22 Rockhopper ....

23 Magellanic ....

24 King ....

Questions 25–27

Write **NO MORE THAN TWO WORDS** *for each answer.*

25 How do penguins usually sleep?

....

26 What do a Rockhopper's yellow feathers do when it is angry?

....

27 What do penguins recognise in the Skua's wings?

....

Questions 28–30

Complete the summary below.

Write **NO MORE THAN TWO WORDS** *for each answer.*

Penguins prefer to swim in groups because it makes it easier to **28** ....
When they are on land, they appear to be **29** .... The majority of
species are characterised by their **30** ...., which makes them particularly
interesting for humans to study.

IELTS TEST 5

Exam Essentials

LISTENING MODULE   READING MODULE   WRITING MODULE   SPEAKING MODULE

SECTION 1
SECTION 2
SECTION 3
SECTION 4

▸ **Questions 31–40**

Complete the sentences below.

Write **NO MORE THAN TWO WORDS** *for each answer.*

31 Governments have been mistaken to ………………………….. slums.

32 There is often a lack of ………………………….. concerning housing projects.

33 Housing policies which are based on principles of …………………………… are particularly effective.

34 Some ………………………………….. should always be provided by governments.

35 Migrants will only ………………………………….. in housing if they feel secure.

36 Governments often underestimate the importance of …………………………………… to housing projects.

37 The availability of …………………………………….. is the starting point for successful housing development.

38 Urbanisation can have a positive effect on the ……………………………………. of individuals.

39 The population size of cities enables a range of ……………………………………. to occur.

40 City living tends to raise the level of …………………………………….. among people.

IELTS
TEST 5

Exam Essentials

| LISTENING MODULE | READING MODULE | WRITING MODULE | SPEAKING MODULE |

PASSAGE 1
PASSAGE 2
PASSAGE 3

*You should spend about 20 minutes on **Questions 1–13**, which are based on Reading Passage 1 on pages 136 and 137.*

Birds' sense of smell

A fascinating ornithological discovery made in recent years is that certain birds – the Starling is one – deliberately place the green foliage of certain aromatic plants in their nests specifically, it appears, to keep parasites such as lice at bay. As though this isn't extraordinary enough, we now know that these birds identify which plants to choose by recognising their smell. This is extraordinary, because until relatively recently it was assumed that most birds have no sense of smell. Apart from vision, which is so obviously excellent in the majority of birds, zoologists have paid relatively little attention to birds' senses. Hearing has very much played second fiddle to sight, not because it is unimportant – it is crucial, given that so many birds communicate by sounds – but because it is difficult to study. As for their other senses: touch, taste and smell, scientists have written birds off as 'insensitive'.

Nothing could be further from the truth. Today there is overwhelming evidence of different kinds that certain birds have an incredible sense of smell. The first line of evidence to be discovered was anatomical. In mammals the front part of the brain holds the 'olfactory bulb.' This is a small piece of tissue that miraculously transforms electrical signals triggered by certain airborne molecules in the nose into something people think of as smell. In some birds the olfactory bulb is relatively large, while in other species it is quite small. Richard Owen, a contemporary of Charles Darwin, was a superb anatomist, and in the 1800s dissected one of the first Kiwi bodies to be brought back from New Zealand to Britain. Owen deduced from the size of its olfactory bulb that the bird must rely on its sense of smell.

Another relevant bit of anatomy is the nasal passages near the base of the bird's beak (their scientific name is conchae). As in humans, these passages comprise delicate scrolls of tissue-covered bone. The more complex the scrolling, the greater the surface area for smell detection. In the 1960s an American woman, Betsy Bang, who was drawing specimens for her anatomist husband, noticed that in three species where there was some behavioural evidence for a sense of smell: the Kiwi, Snow Petrel and the Turkey Vulture, the nasal conchae were much more complex than in other birds.

Evidence for a sense of smell in Turkey Vultures was demonstrated almost by accident. It was assumed that this species finds its carcass prey by smelling them, yet attempts to test this in the early 1800s were rarely successful. This was because it was erroneously assumed that the vultures favoured carcasses which are decomposing and rotten, whereas in fact they avoid these, and are only really interested in fresh ones. New tests proved the point. But what was it the vultures were homing in on? The answer came from an unlikely source. Kenneth Stager, who conducted this research in the 1960s, was talking to technicians who looked after the California gas pipeline. They told him they could tell when there was a leak in the pipe because the Turkey Vultures always congregated around it. It turns out that since the 1930s the company had added a very smelly substance known as mercaptan to the gas to help humans detect leaks, but the birds were infinitely more sensitive to it than people. It also turns out that when an animal such as a deer or cow dies, its body naturally gives off mercaptan - hence the ability of the birds to home in on their food. Stager got hold of some of this substance, blew it across the California hills, and the vultures flocked towards it.

In Europe and Asia there is a bird that appears to have a remarkable ability to smell: the Woodcock. Like the Kiwi, this is a bird that lives predominantly in the dark and finds its food by probing in soft earth or mud. Unlike the Kiwi, the Woodcock has enormous eyes, placed high on its head for all-round vision, because it is vulnerable to predators. The Kiwi, in contrast, originally evolved in a predator-free environment, and gave up both the ability to fly and the ability to see, concentrating on its other senses instead. It can smell earthworms through 15 cm of soil.

The Kiwi's ability to smell has been known for well over a century. In contrast, the Woodcock's olfactory skills have been known for almost two millennia. A poem written in 280 AD refers to the birds' incredible ability to smell worms, and there are several similar independent accounts. An educated traveller, William Bowles, visiting Spain in the 1700s quietly sat and watched a Woodcock foraging in the royal aviaries. The bird simply never missed: it appeared to be able to smell the worm before it stuck its beak into the ground. George Montagu, a British ornithologist, and author of the first Ornithological Dictionary (1802), kept several Woodcocks in his aviary and commented on their remarkable ability to smell food. However, whereas the feeding behaviour of Kiwis has been studied in some detail, so far no-one has conducted a similar investigation of the Woodcock to see how the two compare.

IELTS
TEST 5

Exam Essentials

LISTENING MODULE   **READING MODULE**   WRITING MODULE   SPEAKING MODULE

PASSAGE 1
PASSAGE 2
PASSAGE 3

Questions 1–4

Complete the notes below.

Choose **NO MORE THAN TWO WORDS** *from the passage for each answer.*

Birds' senses

In the past, it was believed that few birds had a sense of smell.

Zoologists used to pay most attention to birds' vision, and less to **1** .... (it is hard to study).

Now there is **2** .... evidence as well as behavioural evidence for a sense of smell:

- Some birds have a large **3** .... (a piece of brain tissue that registers smells).

- The shape of the **4** .... , called conchae, are complex in some birds.

Questions 5–8

Answer the questions below.

Choose **ONE WORD ONLY** *from the passage for each answer.*

5   In what condition are the carcasses which vultures are now known to prefer?

6   Which supplementary ingredient gave a Californian company's fuel its strong smell?

7   In evolutionary terms, what was initially absent from the Kiwi's environment?

8   What can both the Kiwi and the Woodcock detect very accurately?

Questions 9–13

*Look at the following characteristics (**Questions 9–13**) and the list of birds below.*

Match each characteristic with the bird it applies to.

*Write the correct letter **A–D** in boxes 9–13 on your answer sheet.*

List of birds
A Starling
B Kiwi
C Turkey Vulture
D Woodcock

9   It has the ability to see things in a 360° plane.

10 It compensates for its lack of sight with a keen sense of smell.

11 It chooses scented leaves to deter certain insect pests from its nest.

12 Its remarkable sense of smell has been observed and recorded over several centuries.

13 It has proved to be useful in identifying faults in something.

▶ **Questions 14–26**

You should spend about 20 minutes **on Questions 14–26**, *which are based on Reading Passage 2 on pages 141–142.*

Questions 14–20

Reading Passage 2 has seven paragraphs **A–G**.

Choose the correct heading for each paragraph from the list of headings below.

Write the correct number **i–x** *in boxes 14–20 on your answer sheet.*

List of Headings

i	The advantage of an intuitive approach to personality assessment
ii	Overall theories of personality assessment rather than valuable guidance
iii	The consequences of poor personality assessment
iv	Differing views on the importance of personality assessment
v	Success and failure in establishing an approach to personality assessment
vi	Everyone makes personality assessments
vii	Acknowledgement of the need for improvement in personality assessment
viii	Little progress towards a widely applicable approach to personality assessment
ix	The need for personality assessments to be well-judged
x	The need for a different kind of research into personality assessment

---

14 Paragraph **A**

15 Paragraph **B**

16 Paragraph **C**

17 Paragraph **D**

18 Paragraph **E**

19 Paragraph **F**

20 Paragraph **G**

Psychology and personality
ASSESSMENT

A Our daily lives are largely made up of contacts with other people, during which we are constantly making judgments of their personalities and accommodating our behaviour to them in accordance with these judgments. A casual meeting of neighbours on the street, an employer giving instructions to an employee, a mother telling her children how to behave, a journey in a train where strangers eye one another without exchanging a word – all these involve mutual interpretations of personal qualities.

B Success in many vocations largely depends on skill in sizing up people. It is important not only to such professionals as the clinical psychologist, the psychiatrist or the social worker, but also to the doctor or lawyer in dealing with their clients, the businessman trying to outwit his rivals, the salesman with potential customers, the teacher with his pupils, not to speak of the pupils judging their teacher. Social life, indeed, would be impossible if we did not, to some extent, understand, and react to the motives and qualities of those we meet; and clearly we are sufficiently accurate for most practical purposes, although we also recognize that misinterpretations easily arise – particularly on the part of others who judge us!

C Errors can often be corrected as we go along. But whenever we are pinned down to a definite decision about a person, which cannot easily be revised through his 'feed-back', the inadequacies of our judgments become apparent. The hostess who wrongly thinks that the Smiths and the Joneses will get on well together can do little to retrieve the success of her party. A school or a business may be saddled for years with an undesirable member of staff, because the selection committee which interviewed him for a quarter of an hour misjudged his personality.

D Just because the process is so familiar and taken for granted, it has aroused little scientific curiosity until recently. Dramatists, writers and artists throughout the centuries have excelled in the portrayal of character, but have seldom stopped to ask how they, or we, get to know people, or how accurate is our knowledge. However, the popularity of such unscientific systems as Lavater's physiognomy in the eighteenth century, Gall's phrenology in the nineteenth, and of handwriting interpretations by graphologists, or palm-readings by gipsies, show that people are aware of weaknesses in their judgments and desirous of better methods of diagnosis. It is natural that they should turn to psychology for help, in the belief that psychologists are specialists in 'human nature'.

E This belief is hardly justified: for the primary aim of psychology had been to establish the general laws and principles underlying behaviour and thinking, rather than to apply these to concrete problems of the individual person. A great many professional psychologists still regard it as their main function to study the nature of learning, perception and motivation in the abstracted or average human being, or in lower organisms, and consider it premature to put so young a science to practical uses. They would disclaim the possession of any superior skill in judging their fellow-men. Indeed, being more aware of the difficulties than is the non-psychologist, they may be more reluctant to commit themselves to definite predictions or decisions about other people. Nevertheless, to an increasing extent psychologists are moving into educational, occupational, clinical and other applied fields,

IELTS TEST 5

Exam Essentials

LISTENING MODULE   **READING MODULE**   WRITING MODULE   SPEAKING MODULE

PASSAGE 1
PASSAGE 2
PASSAGE 3

where they are called upon to use their expertise for such purposes as fitting the education or job to the child or adult, and the person to the job. Thus a considerable proportion of their activities consists of personality assessment.

F The success of psychologists in personality assessment has been limited, in comparison with what they have achieved in the fields of abilities and training, with the result that most people continue to rely on unscientific methods of assessment. In recent times there has been a tremendous amount of work on personality tests, and on carefully controlled experimental studies of personality. Investigations of personality by Freudian and other 'depth' psychologists have an even longer history. And yet psychology seems to be no nearer to providing society with practicable techniques which are sufficiently reliable and accurate to win general acceptance. The soundness of the methods of psychologists in the field of personality assessment and the value of their work are under constant fire from other psychologists, and it is far from easy to prove their worth.

G The growth of psychology has probably helped responsible members of society to become more aware of the difficulties of assessment. But it is not much use telling employers, educationists and judges how inaccurately they diagnose the personalities with which they have to deal unless psychologists are sure that they can provide something better. Even when university psychologists themselves appoint a new member of staff, they almost always resort to the traditional techniques of assessing the candidates through interviews, past records, and testimonials, and probably make at least as many bad appointments as other employers do. However, a large amount of experimental development of better methods has been carried out since 1940 by groups of psychologists in the Armed Services and in the Civil Service, and by such organizations as the (British) National Institute of Industrial Psychology and the American Institute of Research.

Question 21

Choose **THREE** letters **A–F**.

Write your answers in box 21 on your answer sheet.

Which **THREE** of the following are stated about psychologists involved in personality assessment?

A   'Depth' psychologists are better at it than some other kinds of psychologist.
B   Many of them accept that their conclusions are unreliable.
C   They receive criticism from psychologists not involved in the field.
D   They have made people realise how hard the subject is.
E   They have told people what not to do, rather than what they should do.
F   They keep changing their minds about what the best approaches are.

Questions 22–26

Do the following statements agree with the views of the writer in Reading Passage 2?

In boxes 22–26 on your answer sheet write

YES	if the statement agrees with the views of the writer.
NO	if the statement contradicts the views of the writer.
NOT GIVEN	if it is impossible to say what the writer thinks about this.

22   People often feel that they have been wrongly assessed.

23   Unscientific systems of personality assessment have been of some use.

24   People make false assumptions about the expertise of psychologists.

25   It is likely that some psychologists are no better than anyone else at assessing personality.

26   Research since 1940 has been based on acceptance of previous theories.

IELTS
TEST 5

Exam Essentials

LISTENING MODULE   READING MODULE   WRITING MODULE   SPEAKING MODULE

PASSAGE 1
PASSAGE 2
PASSAGE 3

You should spend about 20 minutes on **Questions 27–40**, *which are based on Reading Passage 3 on pages 144 and 145.*

TITAN of technology

Gordon Moore is one of the people who gave the world personal computers. Peter Richards spoke to him in 2003

Gordon Moore is the scientific brain behind Intel, the world's biggest maker of computer chips. Both funny and self-deprecating, he's a shrewd businessman too, but admits to being an 'accidental entrepreneur', happier in the back room trading ideas with techies than out selling the product or chatting up the stockholders. When he applied for a job at Dow Chemical after gaining his PhD, the company psychologist ruled that 'I was okay technically, but that I'd never manage anything'. This year Intel is set to turn over $28 billion.

When Moore co-founded Intel (short for Integrated Electronics) to develop integrated circuits thirty-five years ago, he provided the motive force in R&D (Research & Development) while his more extrovert partner Robert Noyce became the public face of the company. Intel's ethos was distinctively Californian: laid-back, democratic, polo shirt and chinos. Moore worked in a cubicle like everyone else, never had a designated parking space and flew Economy. None of this implied lack of ambition. Moore and Noyce shared a vision, recognising that success depended just as much on intellectual pizazz as on Intel's ability to deliver a product. Noyce himself received the first patent for an integrated circuit in 1961, while both partners were learning the business of electronics at Fairchild Semiconductor.

Fairchild's success put money in Moore and Noyce's pockets, but they were starved of R&D money. They resigned, frustrated, to found Intel in 1968. 'It was one of those rare periods when money was available,' says Moore. They put in $250,000 each and drummed up another $2.5m of venture capital 'on the strength of a one-page business plan that said essentially nothing'. Ownership was divided 50:50 between founders and backers. Three years later, Intel's first microprocessor was released: the 4004, carrying 2,250 transistors. Progress after that was rapid. By the time the competition realised what was happening, Intel had amassed a seven-year R&D lead that it was never to relinquish.

By the year 2000, Intel's Pentium®4 chip was carrying 42 million transistors. 'Now,' says Moore, 'we put a quarter of a billion transistors on a chip and are looking forward to a billion in the near future.' The performance gains have been phenomenal. The 4004 ran at 108 kilohertz (108,000 hertz), the Pentium®4 at three gigahertz (3 billion hertz). It's calculated that if automobile speed had increased similarly over the same period, you could now drive from New York to San Francisco in six seconds.

Moore's prescience in forecasting this revolution is legendary. In 1965, while still head of the R&D laboratory at Fairchild, he wrote a piece for *Electronics* magazine observing 'that over the first few years we had essentially doubled the complexity of integrated circuits every year. I blindly extrapolated for the next ten years and said we'd go from about 60 to about 60,000 transistors on a chip. It proved a much more spot-on prediction than I could ever have imagined. Up until then, integrated circuits had been expensive and had had principally military applications. But I could see that the economics were going to switch dramatically. This was going to become the cheapest way to make electronics.'

The prediction that a chip's transistor-count – and thus its performance – would keep doubling every year soon proved so accurate that Carver Mead, a friend from Caltech, dubbed it 'Moore's Law'. The name has stuck. 'Moore's Law' has become the yardstick by which the exponential growth of the computer industry has been measured ever since. When, in 1975, Moore looked around him again and saw transistor-counts slowing, he predicted that in future chip-performance would double only every two years. But that proved pessimistic. Actual growth since then has split the difference between his two predictions, with performance doubling every 18 months.

And there's a corollary, says Moore. 'If the cost of a given amount of computer power drops 50 per cent every 18 months, each time that happens the market explodes with new applications that hadn't been economical before.' He sees the microprocessor as 'almost infinitely elastic'. As prices fall, new applications keep emerging: smart light bulbs, flashing trainers or greetings cards that sing 'Happy Birthday'. Where will it all stop? Well, it's true, he says, 'that in a few more generations [of chips], the fact that materials are made of atoms starts to be a real problem. Essentially, you can't make things any smaller.' But in practice, the day of reckoning is endlessly postponed as engineers find endlessly more ingenious ways of loading more transistors on a chip. 'I suspect I shared the feelings of everybody else that when we got to the dimensions of a micron [about 1986], we wouldn't be able to continue because we were touching the wavelength of light. But as we got closer, the barriers just melted away.'

When conventional chips finally reach their limits, nanotechnology beckons. Researchers are already working on sci-fi sounding alternatives such as molecular computers, built atom by atom, that theoretically could process hundreds of thousands times more information than today's processors. Quantum computers using the state of electrons as the basis for calculation could operate still faster. On any measure, there looks to be plenty of life left in Moore's Law yet.

IELTS TEST 5

Exam Essentials

LISTENING MODULE	READING MODULE	WRITING MODULE	SPEAKING MODULE

PASSAGE 1
PASSAGE 2
PASSAGE 3

Questions 27–29

*Choose the correct letter, **A**, **B**, **C** or **D**.*

Write your answers in boxes 27–29 on your answer sheet.

27 What do we learn about Gordon Moore's personality in the first two paragraphs?
   A It has changed noticeably as his career has developed.
   B It was once considered unsuitable for the particular type of business he was in.
   C It made him more suited to producing things than to selling them.
   D It is less complicated than it may at first appear.

28 What do we learn about Intel when it was first established?
   A It was unlike any other company in its field at the time.
   B It combined a relaxed atmosphere with serious intent.
   C It attracted attention because of the unconventional way in which it was run.
   D It placed more emphasis on ingenuity than on any other aspect.

29 What is stated about the setting up of Intel in the third paragraph?
   A It was primarily motivated by the existence of funds that made it possible.
   B It involved keeping certain sensitive information secret.
   C It resulted from the founders' desire to launch a particular product.
   D It was caused by the founders' dissatisfaction with their employer's priorities.

Questions 30–34

Do the following statements agree with the information given in Reading Passage 3?

In boxes 30–34 on your answer sheet write

    TRUE   *if the statement agrees with the information.*

    FALSE   *if the statement contradicts the information.*

    NOT GIVEN *if there is no information on this.*

30 Competitors soon came close to catching up with Intel's progress.

31 Intel's Pentium®4 chip was more successful than Moore had anticipated.

32 Moore's prediction in 1975 was based on too little evidence.

33 Flashing trainers are an example of Moore's theory about the relationship between cost and applications.

34 Moore has always been confident that problems concerning the size of components will be overcome.

Questions 35–40

Complete the summary below using words from the box.

Write your answers in boxes 35–40 on your answer sheet.

MOORE'S LAW

Gordon Moore's ability to foresee developments is well-known. In 1965, he referred to the increase in the **35** .... of integrated circuits and guessed that the number of transistors would go on rising for a decade. The **36** .... of his prediction surprised him. Previously, the **37** .... and main **38** ..... of integrated circuits had been the major **39** .... with regard to their development. But Moore observed that the **40** .... of integrated circuits was going to improve dramatically. His resulting forecasts concerning chips led to the creation of the term 'Moore's Law'.

design	use	opinion	invention
cost-effectiveness	failure	sophistication	proposition
production	influence	understanding	cost
accuracy	demand	theory	inter-dependence
familiarity	reception	appearance	reference

IELTS
TEST 5

Exam Essentials

LISTENING MODULE   READING MODULE   **WRITING MODULE**   SPEAKING MODULE

Task 1

Task 2

You should spend about 20 minutes on this task.

The bar charts and line graph below show the results of a survey conducted over a three-year period to discover what people who live in London think of the city.

Summarise the information by selecting and reporting the main features, and make comparisons where relevant.

Write at least 150 words.

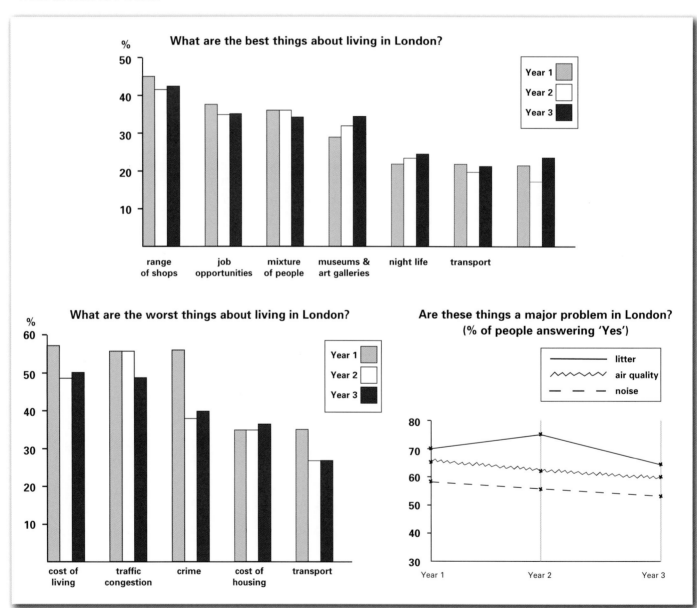

There is a sample answer on page 203.

TEST 5

IELTS

Exam Essentials

LISTENING MODULE   READING MODULE   **WRITING MODULE**   SPEAKING MODULE

Task 1

Task 2

You should spend about 40 minutes on this task.

Present a written argument or case to an educated reader with no specialist knowledge of the following topic.

> *In many countries these days, the number of people continuing their education after school has increased, and the range of courses available at universities and colleges has also increased.*
>
> *Do you think this is a positive or negative development?*

You should use your own ideas, knowledge and experience and support your arguments with examples and relevant experience.

Write at least 250 words.

There is a sample answer on page 203.

▶ PART 1

Example questions

- When did you start to learn English?
- What do you enjoy about learning languages?
- Apart from classes, what are useful ways to practise a language that you are learning?
- How do you plan to use your English in the future?

▶ PART 2

Example task

Read the topic card below carefully.

You will have to talk about the topic for one to two minutes.

You have one minute to think about what you are going to say.

You can make notes if you want.

> **Describe a film you found interesting.**
>
> **You should say:**
> - **when you saw this film**
> - **why you decided to see this film**
> - **what happened in the film**
>
> **and explain why you found this film interesting.**

▶ PART 3

Example questions

- Which do you think is more enjoyable, watching films in the cinema or watching TV programmes?
- Do you think that cinema films should have an educational value?
- Is it important for governments to support film-making in their countries?
- In what ways do you think that entertainment media may develop in the future?

IELTS TEST 6

Exam Essentials

LISTENING MODULE   READING MODULE   WRITING MODULE   SPEAKING MODULE

SECTION 1
SECTION 2
SECTION 3
SECTION 4

▸ **Questions 1–10**

Questions 1–7

Complete the form below.

Write **NO MORE THAN TWO WORDS AND/OR A NUMBER** *for each answer.*

GO-TRAVEL

BOOKING FORM

Name:	1 [Last] .... [First] ....
Source of enquiry:	saw ad in 2 .... Magazine
Holiday reference:	3 ....
Number of people:	4 ....
Preferred departure date:	5 ....
Number of nights:	6 ....
Type of insurance:	7 ....

IELTS TEST 6

Exam Essentials

LISTENING MODULE	READING MODULE	WRITING MODULE	SPEAKING MODULE

SECTION 1
SECTION 2
SECTION 3
SECTION 4

Questions 8–10

Choose **THREE** *letters* **A–H**.

Which **THREE** options does the woman want to book?

    A arts demonstration
    B dance show
    C museums trip
    D bus tour at night
    E picnic lunches
    F river trip
    G room with balcony
    H trip to mountains

8 ....

9 ....

10 ....

LISTENING MODULE	READING MODULE	WRITING MODULE	SPEAKING MODULE

SECTION 1
SECTION 2
SECTION 3
SECTION 4

▶ **Questions 11–20**

Questions 11–17

Complete the notes below.

Write **NO MORE THAN THREE WORDS AND/OR A NUMBER** *for each answer.*

RUN-WELL CHARITY

Background to Run-Well charity
- Set up in **11** ....
- Aim: raise money for the **12** ....

Race details
- Teams to supply own **13** ....
- Teams should **14** .... together
- Important to bring enough **15** ....
- Race will finish in the **16** ....
- Prizes given by the **17** ....

Questions 18–20

Choose **THREE** *letters* **A–H**.

Which **THREE** ways of raising money for the charity are recommended?

A badges
B bread and cake stall
C swimming event
D concert
E door-to-door collecting
F picnic
G postcards
H quiz
I second-hand sale

18 ....
19 ....
20 ....

IELTS TEST 6

Exam Essentials

LISTENING MODULE	READING MODULE	WRITING MODULE	SPEAKING MODULE

SECTION 1
SECTION 2
SECTION 3
SECTION 4

▶ **Questions 21–30**

Questions 21–26

What do the students decide about each topic for Joe's presentation?
A   Joe will definitely include this topic.
B   Joe might include this topic.
C   Joe will not include this topic.

Write the correct letter, **A**, **B** *or* **C** *next to questions 21–26.*

21   cultural aspects of naming people   ....

22   similarities across languages in naming practices   ....

23   meanings of first names   ....

24   place names describing geographic features   ....

25   influence of immigration on place names   ....

26   origins of names of countries   ....

Questions 27–30

Complete the summary below.

Write **NO MORE THAN TWO WORDS** *for each answer.*

Researchers showed a group of students many common nouns, brand names and 27 .... Students found it easier to identify brand names when they were shown in 28 .... Researchers think that 29 .... is important in making brand names special within the brain. Brand names create a number of 30 .... within the brain.

SECTION 1
SECTION 2
SECTION 3
SECTION 4

▶ *Questions 31–40*

Complete the notes below.

Write **NO MORE THAN TWO WORDS** *for each answer.*

Gas balloons

Uses:

• instead of **31** .... in the US civil war

• to make **32** ....

• to **33** .... for research

• as part of studies of **34** ....

Hot air balloons

Create less **35** .... than gas balloons

Airships

Early examples had no **36** .... for crew

To be efficient, needed a

37 ....

Development of large airships stopped because of:

• success of **38** ....

• series of **39** ....

Recent interest in use for carrying

40 ....

IELTS TEST 6

Exam Essentials

| LISTENING MODULE | READING MODULE | WRITING MODULE | SPEAKING MODULE |

PASSAGE 1
PASSAGE 2
PASSAGE 3

You should spend about 20 minutes on **Questions 1–13**, *which are based on Reading Passage 1 on pages 156 and 157.*

How to run a ...

Publisher and author David Harvey
on what makes a good management book

A Prior to the Second World War, all the management books ever written could be comfortably stacked on a couple of shelves. Today, you would need a sizeable library, with plenty of room for expansion, to house them. The last few decades have seen the stream of new titles swell into a flood. In 1975, 771 business books were published. By 2000, the total for the year had risen to 3,203, and the trend continues.

B The growth in pubishing activity has followed the rise and rise of management to the point where it constitutes a mini-industry in its own right. In the USA alone, the book market is worth over $1bn. Management consultancies, professional bodies and business schools were part of this new phenomenon, all sharing at least one common need: to get into print. Nor were they the only aspiring authors. Inside stories by and about business leaders balanced the more straight-laced textbooks by academics. How-to books by practising managers and business writers appeared on everything from making a presentation to developing a business strategy. With this upsurge in output, it is not really surprising that the quality is uneven.

C Few people are probably in a better position to evaluate the management canon than Carol Kennedy, a business journalist and author of *Guide to the Management Gurus*, an overview of the world's most influential management thinkers and their works. She is also the books editor of *The Director*. Of course, it is normally the best of the bunch that are reviewed in the pages of *The Director*. But from time to time, Kennedy is moved to use *The Director*'s precious column inches to warn readers off certain books. Her recent review of *The Leader's Edge* summed up her irritation with authors who over-promise and under-deliver. The banality of the treatment of core competencies for leaders, including the 'competency of paying attention', was a conceit too far in the context of a leaden text. 'Somewhere in this book,' she wrote, 'there may be an idea worth reading and taking note of, but my own competency of paying attention ran out on page 31.' Her opinion of a good proportion of the other books that never make it to the review pages is even more terse. 'Unreadable' is her verdict.

D Simon Caulkin, contributing editor of the *Observer*'s management page and former editor of *Management Today*, has formed a similar opinion. 'A lot is pretty depressing, unimpressive stuff.' Caulkin is philosophical about the inevitability of finding so much dross. Business books, he says, 'range from total drivel to the ambitious stuff. Although the confusing thing is that the really ambitious stuff can sometimes be drivel.' Which leaves the question open as to why the subject of management is such a literary wasteland. There are some possible explanations.

E Despite the attempts of Frederick Taylor, the early twentieth-century founder of scientific management, to establish a solid, rule-based foundation for the practice, management has come to be seen as just as much an art as a science. Once psychologists like Abraham Maslow, behaviouralists and social anthropologists persuaded business to look at management from a human perspective, the topic became more multi-dimensional and complex. Add to that the requirement for management to reflect the changing demands of the times, the impact of information technology and other factors, and it is easy to understand why management is in a permanent state of confusion. There is a constant requirement for reinterpretation, innovation and creative thinking: Caulkin's ambitious stuff. For their part, publishers continue to dream about finding the next big management idea, a topic given an airing in Kennedy's book, *The Next Big Idea*.

F   Indirectly, it tracks one of the phenomena of the past 20 years or so: the management blockbusters which work wonders for publishers' profits and transform authors' careers. Peters and Waterman's *In Search of Excellence: Lessons from America's Best-Run Companies* achieved spectacular success. So did Michael Hammer and James Champy's book, *Reengineering the Corporation: A Manifesto for Business Revolution*. Yet the early euphoria with which such books are greeted tends to wear off as the basis for the claims starts to look less than solid. In the case of *In Search of Excellence*, it was the rapid reversal of fortunes that turned several of the exemplar companies into basket cases. For Hammer's and Champy's readers, disillusion dawned with the realisation that their slash-and-burn prescription for reviving corporate fortunes caused more problems than it solved.

G   Yet one of the virtues of these books is that they could be understood. There is a whole class of management texts that fail this basic test. 'Some management books are stuffed with jargon,' says Kennedy. 'Consultants are among the worst offenders.' She believes there is a simple reason for this flight from plain English. 'They all use this jargon because they can't think clearly. It disguises the paucity of thought.'

H   By contrast, the management thinkers who have stood the test of time articulate their ideas in plain English. Peter Drucker, widely regarded as the doyen of management thinkers, has written a steady stream of influential books over half a century. 'Drucker writes beautiful, clear prose,' says Kennedy, 'and his thoughts come through.' He is among the handful of writers whose work, she believes, transcends the specific interests of the management community. Caulkin also agrees that Drucker reaches out to a wider readership. 'What you get is a sense of the larger cultural background,' he says. 'That's what you miss in so much management writing.' Charles Handy, perhaps the most successful UK business writer to command an international audience, is another rare example of a writer with a message for the wider world.

IELTS TEST 6

Exam Essentials

LISTENING MODULE   **READING MODULE**   WRITING MODULE   SPEAKING MODULE

PASSAGE 1
PASSAGE 2
PASSAGE 3

Questions 1–2

*Choose the correct letter, **A**, **B**, **C** or **D**.*

Write your answers in boxes 1 and 2 on your answer sheet.

1   What does the writer say about the increase in the number of management books published?
    A   It took the publishing industry by surprise.
    B   It is likely to continue.
    C   It has produced more profit than other areas of publishing.
    D   It could have been foreseen.

2   What does the writer say about the genre of management books?
    A   It includes some books that cover topics of little relevance to anyone.
    B   It contains a greater proportion of practical than theoretical books.
    C   All sorts of people have felt that they should be represented in it.
    D   The best books in the genre are written by business people.

Questions 3–7

*Reading Passage 1 has eight paragraphs **A–H**.*

Which paragraph contains the following information?

*Write the correct letter **A–H** in boxes 3–7 on your answer sheet.*

3   reasons for the deserved success of some books

4   reasons why managers feel the need for advice

5   a belief that management books are highly likely to be very poor

6   a reference to books not considered worth reviewing

7   an example of a group of people who write particularly poor books

Questions 8–13

*Look at the statements (**Questions 8–13**) and the list of books below.*

Match each statement with the book it relates to.

*Write the correct letter **A–E** in boxes 8–13 on your answer sheet.*

NB *You may use any letter more than once.*

8 It examines the success of books in the genre.

9 Statements made in it were later proved incorrect.

10 It fails to live up to claims made about it.

11 Advice given in it is seen to be actually harmful.

12 It examines the theories of those who have developed management thinking.

13 It states the obvious in an unappealing way.

> **List of Books**
>
> A *Guide to the Management Gurus*
> B *The Leader's Edge*
> C *The Next Big Idea*
> D *In Search of Excellence*
> E *Reengineering the Corporation*

IELTS
TEST 6

Exam Essentials

LISTENING MODULE   **READING MODULE**   WRITING MODULE   SPEAKING MODULE

PASSAGE 1
PASSAGE 2
PASSAGE 3

You should spend about 20 minutes on **Questions 14–26**, *which are based on Reading Passage 2 on pages 161–162.*

Questions 14–19

Reading Passage 2 has six paragraphs **A–F**.

Choose the correct heading for each paragraph from the list of headings below.

Write the correct number **i–viii** *in boxes 14–19 on your answer sheet.*

List of Headings

i	Modern buildings designed by newcomers
ii	An absence of modern architecture
iii	Britain's modified version of modernism
iv	A supply of suitable building materials
v	The context of modern architecture
vi	The public's reaction to modern architecture
vii	A former source of inspiration for other countries
viii	The basic features of modern architecture

---

    14   Paragraph **A**

    15   Paragraph **B**

    16   Paragraph **C**

    17   Paragraph **D**

    18   Paragraph **E**

    19   Paragraph **F**

EARLY MODERN ARCHITECTURE IN BRITAIN

A Modern architecture is one aspect of Modernism, an umbrella term for a philosophical movement in the arts which arose during the late 19th and early 20th centuries. The movement reflected wide-scale and far-reaching changes in Western society. Among the factors that shaped Modernism was the development of modern industrial societies and the rapid growth of cities. Modernism was also a response to the emphasis of previous centuries on rationalism.

B Modern architecture was generally characterised by simplicity of form and an absence of applied decoration; there was often a visual emphasis on straight lines. In addition, there was a preference for industrially-produced materials, such as steel, concrete and sheet glass, and a tendency to reveal the structural elements of buildings, rather than to conceal them. In a broad sense, early modern architecture began at the turn of the 20th century, with efforts to reconcile the principles underlying architectural design with rapid technological advancement and the modernisation of society.

C In 1931 Berthold Lubetkin, an architect born in Tbilisi, Georgia, travelled to London via Paris. At that time continental Europe sparkled with white concrete and flat roofs, buildings created by architects for whom form followed on from function. But Lubetkin searched in vain for modernist buildings in Britain; there classicism prevailed, interrupted by only an occasional example of art deco design. British architects did use the concrete and steel favoured by modernists, but they covered them over with blocks of limestone. According to Lubetkin, Britain was 'about 50 years behind, as though locked in a deep, provincial sleep.'

D This was especially disappointing for Lubetkin, as he had previously been influenced by British notions of beauty and, like other modernist architects, he had admired the 20th-century English house. The British Arts and Crafts movement had been a catalyst for European modernism. French and German architects had adopted and developed the British emphasis on expressing the nature of materials in a very ambitious way. German architects regarded buildings as 'the spirit of the epoch translated into form.' The French architect, Le Corbusier, controversially insisted that humans needed space, light and order as much as they needed bread, or a place to sleep. In Britain, however, the more radical aims of the Arts and Crafts movement were forgotten after the First World War (1914–1918). Although art deco cinemas sprang up across the country in the 1920s, these frivolous entertainment palaces used modern design as decoration, rather than as a model for a new society.

E It took the arrival of Lubetkin and other immigrants to wrench Britain into the future. For example, Lubetkin provided the country with several modernist masterpieces, including two innovative apartment blocks, and a zoo. Meanwhile Erich Mendelsohn and Serge Chermayeff created the much admired De La Warr Pavilion, a public seaside building on the south coast. In the characteristically modernist style reminiscent of industrial architecture, the streamlined building was devoid of superficial decoration. It featured strong, horizontal lines, with protruding balconies, a curved entrance hall, and large metal-framed windows. The architects rejected traditional brick and stonework in favour of a whitewashed concrete and steel construction. Amongst the building's most innovative features was its use of a welded steel frame construction.

IELTS **T**EST **6**

Exam Essentials

LISTENING MODULE   READING MODULE   WRITING MODULE   SPEAKING MODULE

PASSAGE 1
PASSAGE 2
PASSAGE 3

F   Mass produced steel and concrete were quick to construct and economically attractive, and some British architects went further than their European counterparts, attempting to pour entire buildings from a single mould. But the British liked being cosy, which was hard in modernist open-plan buildings with stark white fronts. As the 1930s progressed, all the arts retreated from the cold abstraction of pure modernism, to produce something more accessible and familiar. The white concrete boxes morphed into a more British version of modernism, dressed in brick and timber. An example of such home-grown modernism are the curved brick tube stations of Arnos Grove and South Wimbledon, designed by Charles Holden. After the Second World War (1939-1945), Britain's version of modernist architecture found expression in a new wave of housing construction, when many people abandoned inner-city flats for suburban houses. For all the great dreams of two generations of imaginative architects and planners, much of Britain remained settled in street-level homes, burrowed in 'provincial sleep'.

Questions 20–23

Do the following statements agree with the information given in Reading Passage 2?

In boxes 20–23 on your answer sheet write

TRUE   *if the statement agrees with the information.*

FALSE   *if the statement contradicts the information.*

NOT GIVEN   *if there is no information on this.*

20   Modernism was a trend associated with industrialisation and urbanisation.

21   At the start of the 20th century, the appearance of modern buildings was usually plainer than that of earlier buildings.

22   When he arrived in Britain, Berthold Lubetkin was favourably impressed by the design of the buildings.

23   During the 1930s, Berthold Lubetkin visited all of Britain's major cities to assess their architecture.

Questions 24–26

Label the diagram below.

*Choose **NO MORE THAN TWO WORDS** from the reading passage for each answer.*

Write your answers in boxes 24–26 on your answer sheet.

THE DE LA WARR PAVILION

Distinctive
26 ....

Metal
Window Frames

24 .... hall

White Washed
Concrete

Overhanging
25 ....

IELTS
TEST 6

Exam Essentials

LISTENING MODULE   READING MODULE   WRITING MODULE   SPEAKING MODULE

PASSAGE 1
PASSAGE 2
PASSAGE 3

You should spend about 20 minutes on **Questions 27–40**, *which are based on Reading Passage 3 on pages 164 and 165.*

The visual language of comics

Neil Cohn's love of comic strips began in his family's attic. In one of his earliest memories, he recalls his dad climbing the stairs and pulling down a box of 1960s Batman and Superman books that he had stashed away from his own childhood. To Cohn's four-year-old self, it was as if they'd been imported from a strange and foreign place. "They had this kind of mystery to them," he says. Instantly he was hooked. It was not long before he became a compulsive comic artist himself; in his teens he even started his own mail-order comic company. As he set about his creations, he would often wonder how the brain makes the huge cognitive leap to piece together a story from the fragmentary, stylised pictures on his drawing board.

Now a psychologist, Neil Cohn is finally getting the chance to answer that question, as he carefully dismantles well-known comic strips. His theory, presented in *The Visual Language of Comics*, is provocative. At a neural level, he says, the pictures of comic strips are processed as another form of language, with their own vocabulary, grammar and syntax. "Human beings only have three ways to convey our thoughts," he explains. "We create sounds using our mouths; we can move our bodies with hands and faces; and we can draw things... My idea is that whenever these meaning-making channels get structured in a coherent sequence, then you end up with a type of language." If he is right, the hidden logic of cartoon panels could provide new vistas on art, language and creative development.

Cohn's theory builds on a growing acceptance that the brain's language toolkit is a kind of multi-purpose piece of equipment for many different kinds of expression, such as music or dance. In some ways the ties with art should be stronger, however – since pictures, unlike music, encode a definite meaning. "Drawing has always been about communication – to express an idea in your head to other people," says Cohn. The drive to tell stories with pictures certainly has deep roots. Stone Age paintings in places such as the *Chauvet* cave in France seem to show scenes of galloping horses and pouncing lions, using techniques that would be familiar to graphic artists today. More advanced picture narratives appeared in works such as the *Bayeux* tapestry and *Paupers' Bibles*. In some indigenous Australian cultures, sand drawings are used as a regular part of discourse; in fact, drawing is so entwined with speech in the language of these cultures that you can't be considered fluent if you don't know the appropriate pictures.

Before Cohn began his research, however, few serious analyses of comic strips existed. One writer who dissected the way strips are constructed was Scott McCloud in his landmark book *Understanding Comics: The Invisible Art*, published in 1993. "That book really got me thinking about it, as a teenager," says Cohn. As part of his university degree in Asian Studies, he decided to take a linguistics course. Suddenly his musings took a whole new shape. "I noticed that all these things that happen in language were the same as the things I understood in comics," he says. Comic strips do, after all, have the basic structure of language, with a hierarchy of elements that can be combined with infinite variety. The building blocks of this hierarchy are a "visual vocabulary" of signs and symbols. That might include speech bubbles, motion lines, or stars to represent the throw of a punch. Even the characters' anatomy is highly stylised: cartoon hands, eyes and noses can look almost identical from strip to strip, even when these are by different artists. "If you look at the bits and pieces, they're all systematic," Cohn says.

At the next level comes the cartoon pane, which combines elements of the vocabulary to build new meanings. It's difficult to find an exact analogy to the English language here; according to Cohn, the cartoon strip pane helps to divide our attention into units, like a word, but it is perhaps closer to the words in agglutinative languages such as Turkish or Inuit, in which stems and suffixes are strung together in a single term to give a more complex meaning. (In one Inuit language, for instance, a single word, *angyaghllangyugtuqlu*, encapsulates the sentence "also, he wants a bigger boat"). Similarly, a single panel of a comic strip can represent a character getting ready to swing his baseball bat through its signs.

Governing the hierarchy is a set of rules that Cohn dubs "narrative grammar". Just as spoken or written grammars contain different types of word – nouns, verbs, adjectives and so on – the narrative grammar includes different types of panel. Among these are: establisher panels, which set up a scene; initial panels, which create a tension; peaks, which show the climax; and release panels, which undo the tension. Each has its own characteristics, and, like the words in a sentence, they have to follow a certain order. Crucially, Cohn argues that these panes can also be grouped into separate clauses that are embedded in larger structures – so a whole string of panels might represent an "establisher" clause in another sequence. That leads to recursion – the property that allows us to say: "He thought that he said that she said…" – which is thought to be one of the defining characteristics of language.

Questions 27–29

Choose **THREE** letters **A–F**.

Write your answers in boxes 27–29 on your answer sheet.

*Which **THREE** of the following issues Neil Cohn considered when studying comics?*

A   the differences between people in their use of art as a means of self-expression
B   how problematic it is to interpret the meaning of comic material from more exotic cultures
C   the details of the process by which a mental narrative is constructed from a sequence of images
D   how similar the reasons for the order of pictures in comics and the way language functions can be
E   the diversity of graphic material employed for the purpose of conveying meaning
F   whether it is possible to achieve fluency in a language through understanding of its art

Questions 30–37

Do the following statements agree with the information given in Reading Passage 3?

In boxes 30–37 on your answer sheet write

> **YES**   *if the statement agrees with the views of the writer.*
>
> **NO**   *if the statement contradicts the views of the writer.*
>
> **NOT GIVEN**   *if it is impossible to say what the writer thinks about this.*

30   Connecting images in comics together allows for endless possibilities.

31   In comics there are notable similarities in certain bodily features.

32   It is necessary to study the brain in order to understand the processes of reading comics.

33   Cohn was influenced by his readings of several in-depth explorations of comic art.

34   Some spoken languages are more suited for use in comics than others.

35   Some aspects of comic creation are hard to compare with linguistic communication.

36   Cohn believes analysis of comics reveals that panels are unconstrained by rules in the way they are organised.

37   Cartoon panels have to use a single image to establish the background to a particular event.

Questions 38–40

Complete the sentences below with words taken from Reading Passage 3.

Use **NO MORE THAN THREE WORDS** *for each answer.*

Write your answers in boxes 38–40 on your answer sheet.

38 The rules that determine the 'grammar' of comics rely on a variety of .... being presented in a particular sequence.

39 In a comic's narrative the scenes showing key dramatic moments are known as ....

40 Among its .... is the fact that language enables ideas to be repeated indefinitely.

You should spend about 20 minutes on this task.

The pie charts below show responses by teachers of foreign languages in Britain to a survey concerning why their students are learning a foreign language. The first chart shows the main reason for learning a foreign language. The second chart shows how many teachers felt that there has been a recent change in the reason.

Summarise the information by selecting and reporting the main features, and make comparisons where relevant.

Write at least 150 words.

% of teachers reporting the following as most common reason for learning:

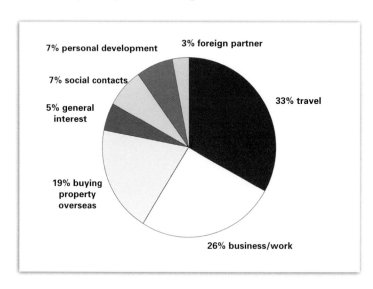

% of teachers reporting recent increase in people learning for the following reasons:

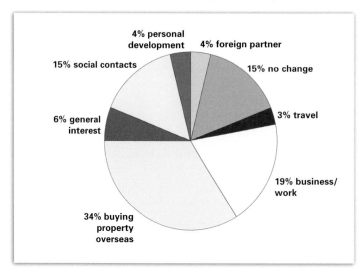

There is a sample answer on page 204.

TEST 6

IELTS

Exam Essentials

LISTENING MODULE   READING MODULE   **WRITING MODULE**   SPEAKING MODULE

Task 1
Task 2

You should spend about 40 minutes on this task.

Present a written argument or case to an educated reader with no specialist knowledge of the following topic.

> *Some people regard work as the most important thing in life and have little interest in anything else. Other people are more enthusiastic about their hobbies and leisure interests than their jobs.*
>
> *Discuss both these attitudes and give your own opinion.*

You should use your own ideas, knowledge and experience and support your arguments with examples and relevant evidence.

Write at least 250 words.

There is a sample answer on page 204.

▸ PART 1

Example questions

- What hobbies and interests are popular in your country?
- Which hobbies or interests do you enjoy?
- Which hobbies or interests did you have when you were a child?
- Do you think parents should encourage their children to have a hobby or interest?

▸ PART 2

Example task

Read the topic card below carefully.

You will have to talk about the topic for one to two minutes.

You have one minute to think about what you are going to say.

You can make notes if you want.

> **Describe the job you most like to have.**
>
> **You should say:**
> - what this job would be
> - where you would work
> - which qualifications you would need
>
> and explain why you would like to have this job most.

▸ PART 3

Example questions
- Which jobs are most respected in your country?
- Do you think schools provide enough advice and support about future careers?
- What changes have there been in recent years in employment in your country?
- Do you agree that pay for a job should reflect the level of contribution to community the job makes?

GENERAL TRAINING MODULE

Tests A and B

▶ **Questions 1–14**

Questions 1–7

Do the following statements agree with the information given in the text on page 173?

In boxes 1-7 on your answer sheet, write

TRUE	*if the statement agrees with the information.*
FALSE	*if the statement contradicts the information.*
NOT GIVEN	*if there is no information on this.*

1 It is best to take your time to find the right place to live.

2 Universities tend to give first year students priority to rent halls of residence.

3 Halls of residence are fairly cheap.

4 Rental contracts for shared accommodation are usually flexible.

5 Student accommodation is often found close to the university.

6 It is a good idea to visit an area you are considering living in to find out more about it.

7 Students should avoid living near noisy neighbours.

Finding student accommodation

On campus or off, the right des-res in your first year needs to be chosen with extra care. Fred Redwood reports.

It can be a difficult task trying to find suitable accommodation if you're going to university far from home, but don't be tempted to make a quick decision. Dr Susan Goddard, the accommodation officer at the University of Reading says: "If you take accommodation in an expensive area or if you move into a flat where you have nothing in common with the other people, you might find you want to move again after a few months. So choose carefully."

How should you go about finding good accommodation? If places in halls of residence are available then it's probably wise to take up one of them. The number of rooms available varies. Reading, which has average provision, gives 48 per cent of students and nearly all first-years the chance of living in hall. A single room with three meals a day should cost about £5,400 for the academic year. It may seem costly, but you will also have an early opportunity to meet other students. However, if you go through Clearing all places in hall may be taken, in which case your first stop should be the accommodation officer.

Dr Goddard says: "Don't give up hope of a room in hall if there isn't one immediately available. Consider living with a host family for a time so you can move quickly if a place becomes free. It will be more difficult to leave a shared flat, where you have to sign a contract and pay a few months' rent in advance."

Another main concern should be convenience. Student accommodation is rarely located in the most central parts of university towns and cities. But you don't want to travel for an hour every day on the bus to get to class.

Ask the accommodation officer which areas are popular with students, and which are the best value for money. It is also a good idea to visit an area at different times of day and in the evening. Is it noisy or quiet? Are there regular buses? Are there good facilities nearby such as shops, a park, or a sports centre?

Think also about your own ability to make noise. You are likely to have parties and, probably, your music collection doesn't contain much in the way of piano sonatas. Find out if the people on the next floor seem likely to appreciate your taste in music and don't live next to an old people's home where people like their peace and quiet.

IELTS
GENERAL TRAINING TEST A

Exam Essentials

READING MODULE   WRITING MODULE

SECTION 1
SECTION 2
SECTION 3

Questions 8–14

*Look at the festival reviews, **A–F**, on page 175.*

For which festival are the following statements true?

*Write the correct letter, **A–F**, in boxes 8–14 on your answer sheet.*

NB *You may use any letter more than once.*

8 It gets more popular every year.

9 It is famous for its internationally themed areas.

10 It is a good place to have a longer holiday.

11 It is popular with many different types of people.

12 Its music is of less importance than other festivals.

13 It is a good place to discover new artists from abroad.

14 It is held in a beautiful area of the UK.

The best summer festivals

Knowing which summer festival to go to and what to do can be a minefield. Read our festival guide and choose one that suits your taste. Natalie Paris reports.

A Wilderness Festival

The main reason to go to this festival is to have fun with friends in a beautiful country setting, with music coming a definite second. In the evening there's entertainment ranging from theatre to huge feasts served at long tables. In the daytime, market stalls sell everything from jewellery to record players and even camel rides.

B Larmer Tree

This summer, organisers are selling seven-day passes that allow holders to arrive early at a dedicated, comfortable campsite and spend a couple of days before the festival exploring the local countryside. Child-friendly, with coastal walks and numerous beaches nearby, for families wanting to take an extended break it could be just the ticket.

C Kendal Calling

Looking at one of the season's most interesting line-ups of bands, any parents of a certain age will recognise the music they loved from the eighties. Set in a deer park in one of Britain's most picturesque regions, Kendal's independent, mid-sized festival wins lots of praise and bigger crowds each summer. Away from the main stage, coffee is served, poetry read and live gigs played to small groups.

D Latitude

With a lakeside surrounded by eye-catching art, a reading area, outdoor theatre and a loud disco in the woods, Latitude really does have something for everyone. The average festival-goers are late teens celebrating exam results or artsy older folk with young families, but who needs trendy people when the atmosphere is this good?

E Great Escape

Each year some of Europe's shiniest new bands set sail for the beaches of Brighton with the intention of gaining new fans. These international acts make the Great Escape unique in the UK and a great place to discover fresh sounds at many of the 30 urban venues around the town.

F BoomTown Fair

BoomTown is less of a festival and more of a weird and wonderful, temporary world, made up of lantern-lit streets leading to different cultural zones. There's a Latin quarter, an American city downtown area, a Chinatown and even an English town hall. One district is accessed via a ski lift and each area boasts great restaurants, bars and discos for late night partygoers.

▸ **Questions 15–27**

Questions 15–21

Read the information about a college's different centres **A–E** *on the following page.*

Write the letters of the appropriate centres in boxes 15–21 on your answer sheet.

NB *You may use any letter more than once.*

Which centre

15 is recommended as a good place for students from abroad?

16 is where courses related to subjects such as nursing are held?

17 is very near to an area where lots of people go shopping?

18 has a new facility for people aiming to work in TV or films?

19 is said to be in a pleasant and attractive area?

20 contains a part that formerly had a different use?

21 has a named area that was specially created to contain certain equipment?

COLLEGE CENTRES

The College has five main Centres:

A Grahame Park Centre

Our Grahame Park Centre offers some of the best training opportunities in North London. It has industry-standard facilities, including hairdressing salons, a construction area, kitchens and a fully functioning training restaurant. The latest addition is a professional media make-up studio with its own photographic area. Our Grahame Park Centre also has superb sports facilities including a 20-metre pool and cardiovascular suite. Naturally, like all our Centres, Grahame Park offers state-of-the-art IT suites all running the latest software. It is also home to the Business Training & Advisory Service (BTAS).

B Montagu Road Centre

With its welcoming, community atmosphere, Montagu Road is a perfect setting for many of the College's international students. Situated in a leafy, residential area, the Centre is close to tube and mainline stations as well as local shops and eateries.

C North London Business Park Centre

The North London Business Park Centre offers a wide-ranging selection of courses, including much of the College's Business & Management and Health & Social Care provision. The Centre has domestic facilities and a horticultural centre for students with special needs. It also houses a working travel agency staffed by Travel & Tourism students. The Centre is served by regular bus routes and has plenty of car parking space.

D Stanhope Road Centre

This small and friendly Centre offers ESOL (English for Speakers of Other Languages), Art & Craft and Adult Basic Skills courses. It is just a short step from busy shopping streets and close to many public transport links.

E Wood Street Centre

Close to all local amenities and with excellent public transport links, this Centre offers courses in varying subjects, and is home to our renowned Art & Design programmes. Facilities at Wood Street include a professional multimedia suite and excellent dance and drama studios. Students have the opportunity to take advantage of the College's extensive IT facilities in the Centre's Belling Suite, a purpose-built unit housing some 50 top-of-the-range PCs. One of the earliest examples of learning in the area can be found at this Centre with the historic Tudor Hall, which was originally opened as a school by Queen Elizabeth 1 in the 16th century.

Questions 22–27

Read the information from the college prospectus on the following page.

Complete the sentences below with words taken from the passage.

*Write **NO MORE THAN THREE WORDS** for each answer.*

Write your answers in boxes 22–27 on your answer sheet.

22 At the .... , college employees are available to give advice at all times.

23 Students should get in touch with the people who run the .... to find out about the Student Union.

24 For people who are interested in discussions, ... are organised.

25 You can visit the .... to find out about Youth & Community Team activities.

26 Paper and pens can be bought in .... at two of the Centres.

27 Students wishing to use the fitness room must do ....

FACILITIES, ACTIVITIES & SPORT

It's not all work, work, work!

We want you to enjoy your time here as well as succeed in your studies. All College Centres have pleasant atmospheres and, when you're not in class, there are plenty of ways to fill your time.

Learning centres

The state-of-the-art learning centres at all our College Centres are carefully designed to optimise self-directed study in a supportive learning environment. There are plenty of networked PCs to work at, with internet access, and a range of other computerised and paper-based resources. Our staff are always on hand to help.

Student Union

The College has an active Student Union, which organises and helps to fund a wide range of activities, represents student opinion to the College management and offers support and advice to its members. Contact the Youth Work team leaders or see the Student Guide for more information.

The Youth & Community Team

This team works with students to organise activities to make your time at the College even more enjoyable and interesting. Some activities complement course work and provide extra accreditation. A programme of actvities runs throughout the year, and usually includes: trips and visits; singing, music and comedy workshops; debates; karaoke and cabaret; yoga and self-defence. Look out for details on College notice boards, or drop into the student common rooms. The Youth Work teams at each College Centre also play a vital part in ensuring the safety and wellbeing of students when they are on College sites.

Food and refreshments

All College Centres offer a selection of refreshments. Grahame Park and Russell Lane provide freshly cooked meals and the other Centres offer a variety of lighter snacks. Grahame Park and Russell Lane also have Poppins shops, which sell a range of items from stationery to confectionery.

Sports

You can enjoy the use of the superb sports facilities at our Grahame Park Centre. There are plenty of arranged activities, and there are drop-in times for you to make use of the facilities at your convenience:

The multi-use sports hall is ideal for a range of activities and exercise classes.

The fitness room is well-equipped with a variety of different resistance and cardiovascular machines to suit most needs. Students wishing to use the equipment must complete an induction course, which can be arranged by a member of staff.

The swimming pool is 20m in length, and regular drop-in times and activities are scheduled. The pool is supervised by a qualified lifeguard. Facilities include showers and changing areas.

IELTS
GENERAL TRAINING TEST A

Exam Essentials

READING MODULE   WRITING MODULE

SECTION 1
SECTION 2
SECTION 3

▸ **Questions 28–40**

Questions 28–33

*The article on pages 181 and 182 has six sections **A–F**.*

Choose the correct heading for each section from the list of headings below.

*Write the correct number **i–x** in boxes 28–33 on your answer sheet.*

List of Headings	
i	Not enough sympathy
ii	The need for action
iii	An inaccurate comparison
iv	Is it really a new phenomenon?
v	The problem gets worse
vi	Not a complete solution
vii	Progress resulting from research
viii	How common is the problem?
ix	Changing attitudes
x	A variety of attempts

     28   Paragraph **A**

     29   Paragraph **B**

     30   Paragraph **C**

     31   Paragraph **D**

     32   Paragraph **E**

     33   Paragraph **F**

RSI

A Pia Enoizi panicked when a specialist told her that she had repetitive strain injury (RSI) and would never be able to work with a computer. Then 19, she was studying history at Cambridge University. 'I saw my career being shot to pieces,' she says. 'What on earth was I going to do? At the time, I was thinking about an academic life.'

The first warning sign was cramp, which struck during a summer job that involved data entry and analysis. 'I sat at the computer on a plastic chair with no thought about posture or taking breaks. One evening, I was cooking pasta and was surprised when I could not lift a pan of boiling water.' The cramps recurred, but she was enjoying the work and put the discomfort out of her mind. Back at Cambridge for her final year, however, she quickly developed essay-writer's cramp. 'We handwrote essays,' says Enoizi, who is now 25. 'First, I found it a struggle to get through a full essay. Next, to my horror, the pain and cramp became so intense I could not write at all. I began to have horrific pins and needles and pains shooting up my arm.'

B More than half a million Britons suffer from RSI – or work-related upper-limb disorder, the description specialists prefer to use. However, this figure includes only reported cases, says Andrew Chadwick, the chief executive of the RSI Association. 'Students and children are not included. Nor are the thousands of stoics who struggle in silence. Many who call our helpline are desperate. They say they cannot afford to lose their jobs.'

RSI is not a diagnosis, but an umbrella term for a range of about 30 painful inflammatory disorders linked to daily overuse of a muscle. Tennis and golfer's elbow are common examples, but many more are occupational. Factory assembly workers and computer users are believed to be the most susceptible, followed by musicians, dressmakers, flight attendants – who repeatedly tear tickets in half – sign language interpreters and litter pickers, who repeatedly squeeze the handles on litter collectors. Text messaging has not yet been known to cause the condition, but Virgin Mobile was concerned enough two years ago to advise users to flex their fingers and shake their wrists occasionally.

C Some specialists draw a parallel between the overuse of muscles and joints by RSI sufferers and the stress suffered by marathon runners. An athlete runs to exhaustion, but would never consider doing so every day; the body needs time to recover before the next event. Yet, with computer-related RSI, the fingers are honed to work faster and faster, says Chadwick: 'It is often the hardest and fastest workers, who put in long hours without proper breaks, who develop a disorder.'

D Enoizi's recovery has taken several years' determination and discipline. She missed a lot of work, but her college paid for an

IELTS
GENERAL TRAINING TEST A
Exam Essentials

READING MODULE   WRITING MODULE

SECTION 1
SECTION 2
SECTION 3

amanuensis – a postgraduate student to whom she dictated essays and her exams papers – and for physiotherapy. But even the repeated dictation led to a painful contraction of the neck muscles. 'During finals, I had to lie on the floor to rest my neck,' she says. Enoizi was delighted to graduate with a first, but she then had to take a year off to rest and retrain her body. Her first stop was a residential chronic pain management course. 'I realised that the damage caused by RSI was never going to go away. I had to learn how to control it.' During her year off, Enoizi visited a chiropractor, an osteopath and a kinesiologist. She also tried magnet therapy and herbal supplements. But none of these made a difference. Pilates, with its emphasis on posture and balancing muscles, helped. Physiotherapy also proved crucial. 'It made a big difference when my physiotherapist bandaged my arms and somehow lifted the forearm muscles away from the nerves. There was an instant feeling of liberation – everything felt less tight.'

E Enoizi now uses a curved keyboard. 'This helps me keep my wrists straight, but with my arms slightly curved, so my elbows do not dig into my ribs. Everything is more relaxed. My chair is fully adjustable and I take frequent breaks.' She is now working at Boots as an assistant project manager. 'I do a mixture of computer analysis, meetings and discussions,' she says. 'But, at the end of a long day, I might get a little pain. I walk briskly – jogging can aggravate joints – stretch gently at my desk and keep up the Pilates. I feel optimistic.'

F Enoizi supports the RSI Association's call for prevention. 'I am concerned about school children,' she says. 'Many use computers for several hours a day, yet are given little advice on posture and injury. Whether they are short, tall, aged 12 or 18, most sit at the same non-adjustable chairs, and at the same height desks. And many send text messages and play games on their computers until late at night.'

Questions 34–39

Complete the summary below using words from the box.

Write your answers in boxes 34–39 on your answer sheet.

What is RSI?

The **34** .... name for RSI is 'work-related upper limb disorder'. The number of people suffering from it is **35** .... , because certain people are not included in the statistics and because for some people the problem is a **36** .... one. RSI is a **37** .... name that includes about thirty unpleasant conditions. Sports people suffer from it, but many other people do as a result of carrying out **38** .... tasks at work. It is not **39** .... whether text messaging can cause it but this is possible.

rising	concerned	general	secret
difficult	false	official	current
likely	complete	constant	characteristic
sure	unknown	clear	routine
simple	flexible	straight	firm

Question 40

*Choose **FOUR** letters A–H.*

Write your answers in box 40 on your answer sheet.

40 Which **FOUR** of the following helped Pia Enoizi?
   A   an amanuensis
   B   an osteopath
   C   magnet therapy
   D   Pilates
   E   physiotherapy
   F   a curved keyboard
   G   brisk walking
   H   jogging

IELTS
GENERAL TRAINING TEST A
Exam Essentials

READING MODULE   **WRITING MODULE**
TASK 1
TASK 2

You should spend about 20 minutes on this task.

> *An Australian friend is coming to visit you, and it will be his/her birthday during the visit.*
>
> *Write a letter to your friend. In your letter*
>
> - *say how you feel about the visit*
> - *suggest what you could do on his/her birthday*
> - *try to find out what you friend thinks of your idea.*

Write at least 150 words.

You do **NOT** need to write your address.

Begin your letter as follows:

Dear .... ,

There is a sample answer on page 205.

IELTS
GENERAL TRAINING TEST A

Exam Essentials

READING MODULE | WRITING MODULE
TASK 1
TASK 2

You should spend about 40 minutes on this task.

You have been asked to write about the following topic.

> *Many young people today are too worried about the way they look and this causes them problems.*
>
> *Do you agree or disagree?*
>
> *What is the situation in your country?*

Give reasons for your answers and include any relevant examples from your experience.

Write at least 250 words.

There is a sample answer on page 205.

IELTS
GENERAL TRAINING T**EST** B   *Exam Essentials*

READING MODULE   WRITING MODULE
       SECTION 1
       SECTION 2
       SECTION 3

▶ **Questions 1–14**

Questions 1–7

Read the extract from a leaflet about walking on the following page and answer Questions 1–7.

Do the following statements reflect the claims of the writer of the leaflet?

In boxes 1–7 on your answer sheet write

YES	*if the statement agrees with the views of the writer.*
NO	*if the statement contradicts the views of the writer.*
NOT GIVEN	*if it is impossible to say what the writer thinks about this.*

1   The Walk for Life scheme has attracted a lot of publicity.

2   Volunteer Leaders have to put in a lot of effort.

3   Some Volunteer Leaders give up the scheme.

4   Taking up regular walking is a simple decision to make.

5   The Walk for Life rewards are meant to be amusing.

6   It is unlikely that many people will complete 100 walks.

7   Everyone who qualifies for a reward according to the records kept will eventually receive one.

WALK for life

Walk for Life is run by the Health and Sports Development Unit of the council. It is part of a national scheme to encourage one million people to walk regularly for their health. The aim is to achieve this by supporting local co-ordinators to develop Volunteer Led Walks.

Walk for Life relies on the hard work and dedication of the Volunteer Leaders. It's not an easy job to please everyone! Week in, week out, whatever the weather, Leaders can be found welcoming new walkers, greeting regulars, completing essential paperwork and ensuring that everyone has a safe walking experience.

For many new walkers, the decision to walk regularly, and more importantly to continue walking, requires motivation, commitment and often involves a major change in lifestyle.

It is often too easy to start a slippery slope by thinking 'I'll just give it a miss this once' when the weather doesn't look very nice or if you are feeling a bit tired.

But **Walk for Life** would like to recognise the fact that you are dedicated and give you a reward to say 'Well done' and act as an incentive to say 'Keep going'!

Once you hit 20 walks you will receive a certificate. After 50 walks you will be able to pull on a Walk for Life cap and feel proud of yourself – that's about one walk every week for a year.

After 75 walks you can be smug in the knowledge that walking with **Walk for Life** is definitely one of your good habits and be safe in the knowledge that after another 25 walks you can look forward to a Mystery Gift.

There may be a delay between reaching a landmark and receiving your reward as some registers are only examined quarterly. Don't worry – just make sure your name is taken down at the start of every walk you attend. Certificates were recently sent to the first Walkers who reached 20 walks and there are many more of you not too far behind! Who will be the first to reach 50 walks?

IELTS
GENERAL TRAINING TEST B

Exam Essentials

READING MODULE   WRITING MODULE
> SECTION 1
> SECTION 2
> SECTION 3

Questions 8–14

Look at the six restaurant reviews, A–F, on page 189.

For which restaurant are the following statements true?

Write the correct letter, **A–F***, in boxes 8–14 on your answer sheet.*

You may use any letter more than once.

8 It may be necessary to wait to get a table.

9 It is best to choose from the menu that changes daily.

10 It could be difficult to stick to a budget when eating here.

11 It serves dishes devised from mixing different cooking styles.

12 It is likely to make customers want to return for a special dish.

13 It is open from morning until late in the evening.

14 It serves some of its best food at the beginning of the week.

WHERE TO EAT FOR LESS IN NEW YORK

Our New York expert recommends the best dining options for under £20.

Lucien

A You may you not be able to order whatever you like on the menu at this popular restaurant in the East Village and come out spending under £20, but it's worth a visit for the food and atmosphere. We recommend the steak and chicken dishes, which are particularly good value.

Marlow & Sons

B This is a small wood-panelled space that's a coffee shop by day, and a restaurant and bar by night. Dishes served from the small menu are made from fresh ingredients and the desserts created by the in-house pastry chefs are really worth tasting. You can even buy one to take home with you from their shop next door which specialises in a wide range of handmade products.

Fragole

C This traditional Italian in a trendy part of Brooklyn, is not as famous as some others nearby, but its home-made pastas and fresh sauces draw in a young, fashionable crowd of knowledgeable foodies. There are plenty of classic dishes, but you won't be disappointed if you opt for the specials which are different everyday.

Dos Toros Taqueria

D This is Mexican food made from super-fresh ingredients, with friendly service and in funky surroundings. The menu is a simple list of burritos, tacos and quesadillas. I defy anyone who has tasted the guacamole-filled grilled chicken quesadilla not to come back for more.

Abboccato

E The aroma of freshly baked breads draws you into this elegant Italian in the unlikely setting of Midtown. The pastas are handmade and regional dishes include seafood which is best on a Monday. It's also far less busy early in the week than on the weekends.

Mission Chinese Food

F This is the second restaurant created by the Korean-born chef, who combines Chinese, Korean and Western traditions with his unique culinary skills. It's often packed so you might not be seated straight away. The menu changes regularly and the service is speedy. It's best to order a mix of spicy and mild dishes and share with your dinner date.

IELTS
GENERAL TRAINING TEST B

Exam Essentials

READING MODULE   WRITING MODULE

SECTION 1
SECTION 2
SECTION 3

▶ *Questions 15–27*

Questions 15–20

Read the information from a college prospectus on the following page and complete the flow charts below.

Use **NO MORE THAN THREE WORDS** *from the passage for each answer.*

Write your answers in boxes 15–20 on your answer sheet.

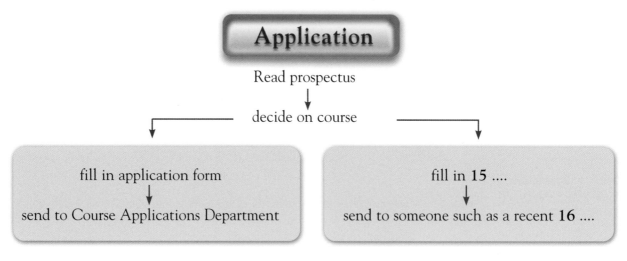

Application

Read prospectus

↓

decide on course

fill in application form	fill in **15** ....
↓	↓
send to Course Applications Department	send to someone such as a recent **16** ....

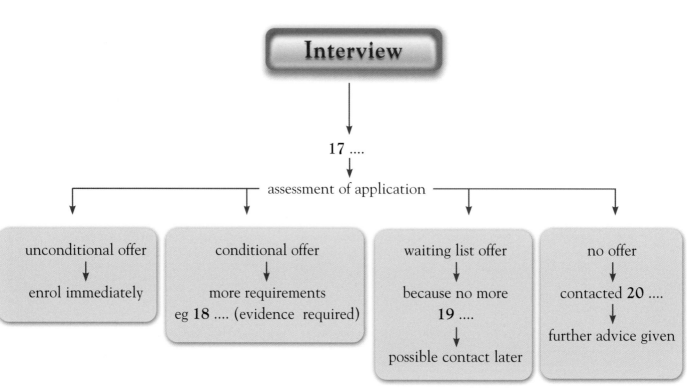

Interview

↓

17 ....

↓

assessment of application

unconditional offer	conditional offer	waiting list offer	no offer
↓	↓	↓	↓
enrol immediately	more requirements eg **18** .... (evidence required)	because no more **19**	contacted **20** ....
		↓	↓
		possible contact later	further advice given

APPLICATION & INTERVIEW INFORMATION

Application

After you have read through the prospectus and decided which course you want to apply for, please follow the simple procedures detailed below:

1 Detach and complete the centre-fold application form and return it as soon as possible to:
Course Applications Department, The Admissions Centre, Southgate College, High Street, Southgate, London N14 6BS

2 Complete and forward the reference form to someone who knows of you and your progress. This person would usually be your present or last tutor.

Interview

After we have received your application and reference form, you will be invited in for an interview, during which you will be taken on a tour of the College, and we will assess your application to ensure we offer the right course for you.

After Interview

Unconditional offer

If you have already achieved the entry requirements to join the College, an 'unconditional offer' will be given to you and arrangements will be made for you to enrol as soon as possible.

Conditional offer

You will be given a 'conditional offer' if there are additional criteria to be met; these may include exam results or further practical tests or reports. On receipt of your exam results, you will need to show the College evidence of your grades.

Waiting list offer

If the course of your choice is oversubscribed and there are no longer any places available, you may be included on the 'waiting list', either with a conditional or an unconditional offer. We will then contact you with an offer if a place becomes available.

No offer

If, after the interview, the College considers that you will not benefit from the course of your choice, we will contact you in writing and will offer further advice on your next step.

IELTS
GENERAL TRAINING TEST B *Exam Essentials*

READING MODULE	WRITING MODULE

SECTION 1
SECTION 2
SECTION 3

Questions 21–27

Read the information about student services at a college on the following page.

Complete each sentence with the correct ending A–J from the box below.

Write the correct letter A–J in boxes 21–27 on your answer sheet.

21 People who are not currently students at the college can find out about courses from

22 Students with problems in their private lives can speak to

23 Students collecting material for a piece of course work can get help from

24 Students having problems with their course may be advised to speak to

25 People trying to decide which course would be best for them should speak to

26 Someone who only wants a brief chat about jobs can go without an appointment to

27 A student may be offered a specially created way of solving their problem by

---

A   a personal tutor.

B   the Prospects Careers Service.

C   the Inclusive Learning Support Manager.

D   the Progression Centre.

E   an examinations officer.

F   the Library and Learning Resources Centre.

G   the College Youth Worker.

H   someone in the Admissions Centre.

I   someone who is not a member of the college staff.

J   a Careers Officer.

STUDENT SERVICES

A wide range of facilities and services is available at the College to assist you with your studies and to help you overcome difficulties. The following is a flavour of what we can offer.

Information

The Admissions Centre provides information about all the College's courses and learning programmes. The staff are here to give you opportunities to discuss your education and training needs and to match them with the right course.

Careers

As well as offering drop-in sessions for quick queries and advice, Prospects Careers Service also provides individual advice and guidance about education, training, career and employment opportunities. You can book an appointment with a Careers Officer in the Progression Centre.

Progression Centre

The Progression Centre aims to help our students and the local community find out more about the opportunities available to them and to help them achieve their next move in education or employment. Students can drop in or book an appointment for advice or opportunities available.

Library & Learning Resources

Our Library & Learning Resources Centre provides a state-of-the-art learning environment offering information and resources to help you succeed. Our specialist team are here to support an appropriate

learning environment and to guide you through information-gathering tasks for assignments. A large suite of computers allows access to a wide range of information-based software.

Learning Support

The Inclusive Learning Support Service is available for any student who is having difficulties with their coursework. The Inclusive Learning Manager will see any student for a guidance interview to develop a support programme based on individual need. The support may be on a one-to-one basis with a member of the Inclusive Learning Support team or from outside agencies. The service also applies to examination boards on behalf of students who require concessions due to a disability and/or learning difficulty.

Counselling and Student Services

The Co-ordinator of Student Services, the College Youth Worker and the Nursing Welfare Officers provide information, advice, support and personal counselling on any issues that may cause difficulties or worry.

IELTS
GENERAL TRAINING TEST B

Exam Essentials

READING MODULE   WRITING MODULE

SECTION 1
SECTION 2
SECTION 3

▶ *Questions 28–40*

Read the following passage and answer Questions 28–40.

Natural assets worth saving in the Outback

John Craven meets the conservationist who believes every endangered creature must have its price

A What's the going rate for a hairy-nosed wombat? How much for a yellow-footed rock wallaby? It's hard to believe, but some of Australia's most endangered species are now listed as assets in the annual balance sheet of one of the country's top companies. Earth Sanctuaries Ltd says it is revolutionising conservation by applying the rules of private enterprise to its eight wildlife reserves ... and every animal it protects has a price tag. By the year 2025, the company aims to have turned one per cent of the continent into places where vanishing native species are safeguarded behind high fences.

B For visitors like me, staying in the basic but comfortable sanctuaries and enjoying escorted walks through the bush is a wonderful way of discovering what Australia was like before the Europeans arrived two centuries ago and changed everything. Under the southern stars, beams of powerful torches capture an array of weird and wonderful creatures as they bounce along – most of the inhabitants are nocturnal marsupials. Many I'd never heard of, such as bilbies, potoroos, bandicoots, rufous bettongs and woylies, which – at just a few inches high – are the world's smallest and rarest kangaroos.

C They are also worth a small fortune, according to Earth Sanctuaries, which has, for example, 38 bilbies, 20 more than last year, with a value of £80,000. Those hairy-nosed wombats are worth £525 each and the market price of its 120 rock wallabies is £125,000. They are among 1,189 creatures, worth more than £1.6 million, which have gone on the books of Earth Sanctuaries now that Australian companies can value 'non-human living organisms held for commercial purposes' as assets.

D As I walked through the showpiece sanctuary at Warrawong, in the hills above Adelaide in South Australia, several hundred thousand pounds worth of rare marsupials scattered before me. My guide was managing director John Wamsley, a giant of a man who created Warrawong after making his fortune in the building industry. He spent much of his money and 12 years of his time turning a dairy farm into a landscape which the first European settlers would have recognised – while also teaching maths at the local university.

E 'Then I hit on the idea of making it into a business,' John told me. 'Earth Sanctuaries has to raise nearly half a billion pounds in the next 25 years. As a charity, there's no way we could do that, but it's a trivial amount in the marketplace. We sold shares in the company, using our land and animals as assets. Share values have increased one hundredfold in 14 years, which I think is better than any other company in Australia. And there are 12 species of rare or endangered animals that have grown in numbers because of us. When we listed on the Stock Exchange, we were the first publicly-listed company in the world with conservation as its core business, but I'm sure that in years to come, conservation companies will be everywhere. It's an ideal, incredibly simple way to raise funds.'

F From its beginnings at Warrawong, Earth Sanctuaries is now an £8 million company with a quarter of a million acres of land and eight sanctuaries, each unique. Warrawong, for instance, has at least 20 duck-billed platypuses living in the swamps and ponds that John Wamsley dug out personally. At Yookamurra, 90 minutes' drive from Adelaide, nine miles of 'feral' fencing – keeping out foxes, cats and so on – protects 3,000 acres of mallee trees that are home to near-extinct species such as the numbat. More than a hundred of these delicate, termite-eating marsupials live in the hollows of 1,000-year-old mallees. And John Wamsley says: 'So how can I spend shareholders' money saving the oldest forest in Australia? On the face of it I can't, because the wood is worthless. But now that it has £260,000 worth of numbats living in it, I have to save it because, if I lose those numbats, I'm not looking after my shareholders' assets.'

G And these appealing little animals with extremely long noses are valuable assets – John recently sold half a dozen to the West Australian government for more than £2,000 each. To catch sight of one – something few people have done – I had to keep watch for an hour or so at dawn in absolute silence. Suddenly one appeared, followed quickly by three others – long noses twitching, spikey tails high in the air. For a few minutes they played around the tree before scampering off in search of a termite breakfast. Once, numbats ranged across the whole of southern Australia. Now they are down to a few hundred – and I had just seen four of them. That's what eco-tourism should be all about.

H Before the sanctuary was established, Yookamurra was dying – now it teems with wildlife, some of it quite tame. Wilma the wombat, all muscle and action, trundles between the bush and the tourist huts like a hairy tank. She looks cute but it's best not to get too close because, like her relative the koala, she has quite a bite. Emus and their chicks wander unconcerned past the restaurant terrace, while a small mob – that is their collective noun – of kangaroos hangs around quite shamelessly hoping for titbits.

I The newest and largest sanctuary is Scotia, a £4 million project covering 150,000 acres of the Outback of New South Wales. The world's longest feral fence has just been built to guard creatures such as bridled nail-tailed wallabies, stick nest rats (really appealing animals – honest!) and brush-tailed bettongs.

IELTS
GENERAL TRAINING **TEST B**   *Exam Essentials*

READING MODULE   WRITING MODULE
             SECTION 1
             SECTION 2
             SECTION 3

Questions 28–33

The passage has nine paragraphs labelled **A–I**.

Which paragraph contains the following information?

Write the correct letter **A–I** *in boxes 28–33 on your answer sheet.*

28 a change in rules concerning companies in Australia

29 a term used for a group of a particular creature

30 a business deal made with another organisation

31 a belief that other organisations like Earth Sanctuaries will be set up

32 a creature that can be dangerous if approached by humans

33 sources of light for seeing creatures

Questions 34–39

Classify the following statements as referring to

      W *Warrawong*
      Y *Yookamurra*
      S *Scotia*

Write the correct letter, **W**, **Y** *or* **S** *in boxes 34–39 on your answer sheet.*

34 It contains something of no financial value.

35 It contains places for visitors to stay in.

36 It is the most recently created sanctuary.

37 It contains creatures that are said to be more attractive than their name suggests.

38 It was formerly used for a different kind of business.

39 It contains areas of water created by the founder.

Question 40

Choose the correct letter, **A**, **B**, **C** *or* **D**.

Write your answer in box 40 on your answer sheet.

40   Which of the following best summarises the writer's attitude in the passage?
    A   He is doubtful about the approach being taken by Earth Sanctuaries.
    B   He is surprised by how little he knew about endangered species.
    C   He is impressed by what is being achieved by Earth Sanctuaries.
    D   He is amazed that John Wamsley's ideas have not been tried before.

IELTS
GENERAL TRAINING TEST B

Exam Essentials

READING MODULE | **WRITING MODULE**
TASK 1
TASK 2

You should spend about 20 minutes on this task.

> *You recently visited a tourist attraction and you were very pleased by the help given to you by the staff.*
>
> *Write a letter to the head of staff at the tourist attraction. In your letter*
>
> • *give details of the circumstances of your visit*
> • *describe the help given to you by the staff*
> • *say what you want the head of staff to do.*

Write at least 150 words.

You do **NOT** need to write your address.

Begin your letter as follows:

Dear Sir or Madam .... ,

There is a sample answer on page 206.

IELTS
GENERAL TRAINING TEST B

Exam Essentials

READING MODULE   WRITING MODULE

TASK 1

TASK 2

You should spend about 40 minutes on this task.

You have been asked to write about the following topic.

> *Some people think that young people should be ambitious. Others believe that it is fine if young people do not have big aims in life.*
>
> *Discuss both these views and give your own opinion.*

Give reasons for your answer and include any relevant examples from your experience.

Write at least 250 words.

There is a sample answer on page 206.

▸ **Test 1**

Task 1 (*page 44*)

The charts show that the number of people who speak a regional language to their children is a great deal lower than the number of people whose parents spoke a regional language to them. For example, over 600,000 people had parents who spoke Alsatian to them habitually and over 200,000 had parents who spoke it occasionally, but only 400,000 speak it to their children now. The fall is even greater in the case of Occitan. Over 600,000 people had parents who spoke this language to them habitually and over 1 million who spoke it to them occasionally, but the number of those people who speak the language to their own children is just over 200,000. In the case of Breton, over 200,000 people had parents who spoke it to them habitually and almost 400,000 had parents who spoke it occasionally, but now under 100,000 people speak it to their own children. There has not been much decrease in the numbers for Creole and Corsican, but these were not as high as the others before. The overall picture presented by the charts is that people are not passing on regional languages to their children as much as they used to.

Task 2 (*page 46*)

These days, stress is a big subject. In all sorts of jobs, people get ill because of it and have time off work. The business world is full of pressure and many people are worried all the time that they might lose their jobs if they don't work harder and harder. Lots of people work very long hours and are given very difficult targets to meet. Their employers expect a lot and sometimes they cannot cope. Young people suffer from stress too – for example, when they have to take exams that will have a big effect on their future. And in general, life is more stressful for a lot of people than it used to be because everything is faster than it used to be. People are always in a hurry to do everything and the pace of life has increased.

But is life really more stressful than it used to be? In the past, people didn't have the comforts that they have now. They had to do a lot more things for themselves. They didn't have all the equipment that people take for granted now, like heating and fridges and microwave ovens and washing machines and telephones and cars. Life was harder for most people. Working conditions for an enormous number of people were much worse than they are today, when a lot of the difficult manual work is done by machines.

The impression I have from talking to older people is that they simply accepted that life was hard and they didn't complain of suffering from stress. They simply got on with their lives. These days there are all sorts of 'experts' talking about how much stress people have – people didn't talk about this in the past.

In my opinion, people today have different pressures from the ones they had in the past, but this does not mean that they have more pressures. In the past, people had harder lives in many ways. It has become fashionable to talk about stress, but it's not a new thing – the difference is that nowadays people complain or become ill because of it, whereas in the past they didn't.

▶ Test 2

Task 1 (page 84)

The table shows that the small companies considered the best to work for have some things in common but also differ greatly in some aspects. In terms of staff numbers, the figures are fairly similar, although the fifth company has a much higher number of staff than the other four.

The best company has a high proportion of female staff, and the fourth best company an even higher proportion of female staff. However, this is not the case for the other companies, and the third company has far more male than female members of staff. As for age of staff, three of the companies have a high proportion of people aged under 35, but the fourth company has a low percentage in that age group. All the companies have no members of staff or only a small percentage aged over 55. The best company has a comparatively low staff turnover figure of 5% and the third company's figure for this is also low at 8%. However, the figure is much higher for the other companies, and the fifth best company has a very high staff turnover of 33%. With regard to salaries, the top company has about a third of staff earning high incomes, the second company has about half and the third company about three-quarters. However, for the other two companies the figure is extremely low.

The overall picture is that, apart from the lack of people in the older age group, there are no consistent features that make a small company popular with its staff. Even salaries do not always seem to be a major factor.

Task 2 (page 86)

People know a lot more about other countries today than they used to. First of all, they can travel there much more easily than they could in the past. You can fly to almost anywhere and air travel is a lot more affordable for many people than it used to be. As a result, more and more people have personal experience of other countries, and they see for themselves how other people live. In some ways, this is a good thing because it helps people of different nationalities and from different cultures to understand each other much better. They have more understanding of each other and this helps people to get on better together.

The media also show people about how others live. People have much more access to international news than they used to, both in newspapers and on television. Satellite television enables people to see programmes from other countries and the internet also gives people access to what is going on all over the world. People are much more informed about other countries. This kind of knowledge is a very useful thing because it can make people change their own attitudes. People in one country can learn a lot about what happens in other countries and use this knowledge to do things differently in their own country.

However, there are disadvantages too. International travel can cause problems when people from richer countries visit poorer countries in large numbers. The people in the poorer countries, though they might make some money, often dislike the attitudes of the visitors. Visitors often make little effort to meet the local people, or treat them as inferiors, and so international travel can cause problems between people rather than increased understanding. A disadvantage of the spread of mass media is that it can make people jealous of how people in richer countries live. If they see rich people living lives of luxury in TV programmes, whereas their own lives are difficult, they may dislike these people. And access to international news may cause problems too because people may decide that they dislike other countries that they knew nothing about before.

In conclusion, I would say that there are both big advantages and disadvantages of these developments. On the whole, I think that the advantages outweigh the disadvantages because the spread of international travel and mass media has led to greater understanding between nations and cultures, and this has been one of the best developments in the world in modern times.

▶ Test 3

Task 1 (page 108)

> The first graph shows that 200,000 drivers were caught speeding in the first year of speed cameras. After that, the number rose steadily until the fifth year, when it began to rise dramatically. Between the fifth and eighth years, it rose from about 450,000 to over 1.5 million. However, the number of road accident fatalities over the same period hardly changed at all. Although it fell slightly during the fourth year, it remained fairly constant at just over 3,000 per year. It would therefore appear that giving people fines for speeding had no effect on the number of serious road accidents. This is the view of the people in the survey. The majority of them felt that speed cameras did not reduce the number of road accidents, and 71% of them felt that the purpose of them was to get money from fines, rather than to improve road safety. Just over half thought that there were too many speed cameras, and the rise in the number of fines indicates that more and more cameras were installed over the eight-year period.

Task 2 (page 109)

> I don't agree that genuine talent is not valued or appreciated these days. The difference is that people nowadays have access to technology that can enable them to create things they could not have done on their own in the past. As a result, some very talented people whose work nobody would have seen or heard in the past are able to become well-known.
>
> This is particularly true in popular music, where the 'anyone can do it' attitude has always been an important feature. In recent times, computer technology has been invented, which makes it possible for people to create and record their own music at home, with very high quality of sound. They don't have to pay to go to expensive recording studios and because of digital equipment, they can make the sound of a whole group without needing a lot of other musicians. Some very talented people have become rich and famous as a result of making their first recordings at home in this way.
>
> Of course, some people with absolutely no talent do become rich and famous. Some very poorly written books become best sellers, some people with no apparent artistic ability become famous artists and some people who cannot act at all become television stars. The idea that you need special gifts and skills and that you need to train and practise a lot has disappeared in some areas of the arts. There is now a belief that ordinary people who are just like everyone else can succeed, whereas in the past people in the arts were seen as special in some way and admired because they could create things that most people could not. However, in my opinion, genuine talent is still admired. People with no talent do become rich and famous but people still appreciate and value genuine talent.

▸ Test 4

Task 1 *(page 128)*

To build a water clock, you must first get a stand and attach a bottle at the top of it with some tape. This bottle must have a hole in the bottom of it and a hole at the side, into which you glue a straw. Then you get another bottle, cut the neck off it and place it beneath the first bottle.

You begin the process by turning the tap on and covering the hole at the bottom of the first bottle with your finger. Water drips from the tap into that bottle until it is full and water overflows through the straw. This keeps a constant level of water in the bottle. Then you take your finger away from the hole, so that water drips through it and into the second bottle. As it drips into the second bottle, you mark with a pen on the second bottle what the level of water is after one minute, after two minutes, and so on. When the second bottle is full and you have made marks for each minute, you empty the second bottle. You can then repeat the process to time things, for example because you know how many minutes it takes for all of the water to pass from the top bottle to the bottom bottle.

Task 2 *(page 129)*

Many older people are forced to end their working lives much earlier than they would like to, and this is a shame because their experience is valuable. Also, it is good for people to work if they want to. If more older people were able to get good jobs, it would be good for business, the economy and society.

One reason why older people find it difficult to get good jobs is that many jobs these days require skills and knowledge that they did not get when they were younger. In particular, computers and information technology play a very big role in many professions, and these are things that only came into existence after older people had finished school or college and after they had begun their working lives.

Another reason is that in many countries these days, there is a view that younger people are preferable for many jobs to older people. Experience is seen as being less important than youth. Many businesses and industries have a majority of workers who are young, and young people are promoted to top jobs much more quickly than they used to be. One way of solving the problem is for older people to be re-trained so that they learn the skills required in the modern world. Training courses should be made widely available and affordable. Older people should be made to feel that they can get good jobs after re-training, and this will encourage them to re-train. Employers should understand that older workers have a lot to offer, and that their experience can be very useful to companies, for example because they can pass their experience of work and life on to younger employees.

▸ **Test 5**

Task 1 *(page 148)*

The first chart shows that the most popular aspects of living in London were the range of shops, the job opportunities and the mixture of people, followed by museums and art galleries, nightlife, transport and parks. The percentage of people naming these things hardly changed at all over the three years of the survey, although the number of people naming shops and job opportunities fell slightly, and the number of people naming museums and art galleries, nightlife and parks went up slightly.

The second chart shows that the cost of living and traffic congestion were seen as the worst aspects of life in London, followed by crime, the cost of housing and transport. However, the percentage of people choosing these aspects fell over the three years in all cases apart from housing. It is interesting to notice that transport was seen as both one of the best and one of the worst things about living in London.

With regard to major problems, the percentage of people who felt that air quality, noise and litter were major problems fell over the three years, although it rose slightly in the second year for air quality. The overall view given by the charts is that people felt that there were improvements with regard to most things they disliked about living in London over the three years.

Task 2 *(page 149)*

Most people would say that education is a good thing, and therefore that it is a positive development that more and more people are continuing their education after they leave school. A more educated population must have a positive impact on a country, in both economic and social terms.
From the point of view of the people themselves, they have more choice as to what they can do, and this must also be a positive thing. People can now study subjects that really interest them, rather than subjects they had to do because there was less choice, and they can also study more subjects that are directly related to the kind of work they want to do. There are many more specialised courses on offer that qualify people for specialised jobs.

On the other hand, lots of people these days do courses that may be regarded as a bit silly. You can do courses in all sorts of things that have no connection with jobs and that cannot be taken seriously as academic subjects. I have heard of people doing degrees in subjects like pop music, and it is hard to see how useful such courses and qualifications are. Also, many people now do subjects such as media studies because a lot of young people want to work in the media. However, there are not that many jobs available for these people, and so a lot of them have simply wasted their time doing a degree in a subject that does not help them to get a job.

In general, I think that the increase in people continuing their education after school and the increase in the range of courses available to them is both a positive and a negative development.

▶ **Test 6**

Task 1 (*page 168*)

The first chart shows that, according to teachers, the most common reason why people learn a foreign language is travel, with business and work being another major reason. 19% of teachers said that buying property overseas is the main reason. General interest, social contacts, personal development and having a foreign partner were other, less common reasons.

The second chart indicates recent changes in the reasons why people learn a foreign language. The biggest change is in people learning because of buying property overseas, with 34% of teachers saying that the number of people learning for this reason has increased. The next biggest increase is in the number of people learning for business and work, with a similar increase in the number learning for social reasons. About the same number of teachers report no change in the reasons for learning. According to teachers, the number of people learning for travel has not increased much, and there has also not been much increase in the number of people learning because of general interest, having a foreign partner or personal development.

The charts therefore indicate that more British people are buying property overseas and this is why they are learning a foreign language.

Task 2 (*page 169*)

Some people live for their work. They are obsessed by it and they work and work. Workaholics like this often experience health problems after a while because they do not rest or eat properly and they are in a permanent state of stress. They do not know how to relax and they do not know how to enjoy life. This surely cannot be a good thing. However, some people whose job is the most important thing in their lives are perfectly happy. If you are lucky enough to have a job that you love, doing it all the time is not exhausting or problematic because you enjoy it all the time. People who have careers that make them happy do not need hobbies and leisure pursuits for relaxation - they are happy and satisfied anyway.

Of course it is true that most people have to earn a living and that, unfortunately, this often involves doing a job that you don't enjoy. Lots of people have jobs they hate or that they find very boring or depressing. For such people, hobbies and leisure pursuits are extremely important. They provide something to look forward to at the end of a working day or week, and they provide something that people can give all their enthusiasm and attention to. For example, a big interest in playing or watching sport allows people to forget their jobs and other problems for a while and concentrate fully on something that is simply enjoyable. Hobbies that may seem strange to other people can also give people something they can focus their energies and thoughts on.

In my opinion, hobbies and leisure pursuits are vital. You shouldn't think only about work. You need a balance in your life, you need something that offers simple pleasure and compensates for the unpleasant aspects of work. Some people don't need this because their jobs are also a pleasure for them, but I don't know any people like that!

▶ General Training Module: Test A

Task 1 *(page 184)*

Dear Shane,

I'm really looking forward to your visit here next month, and I hope you'll have a great time meeting my friends and family. There are lots of interesting places I can show you in the area, and there are plenty of places we can go in the evenings to have fun.

I've just realised that it'll be your birthday while you're over here, won't it? I've been thinking about what we could do that day. I think it would be a great idea if we went to the Adventure World theme park, which isn't far from where I live. I haven't been there myself, but friends tell me it's a fantastic place for a day out. It's got some really exciting rides, apparently, including one called The Shake-Up, which everyone talks about when they've been there.

Let me know what you think. I know you like a bit of excitement, and it would be easy for us to get there. Do you fancy it? If so, I can start organising the trip. If it's not the sort of thing that appeals to you, I'll think of something else. If you have a better suggestion, let me know and I'll try to organise that.

Love,

Helena

Task 2 *(page 185)*

I think it is true that many young people worry too much about the way they look. Certainly, I think this is true where I come from. For example, a lot of girls in my country worry about being too fat and they are always on a diet of some sort. They get the idea that they ought to be thin from magazines and celebrities and this can cause them problems. Even people who aren't really fat think that they are. Sometimes this can make them ill, because they can develop eating disorders. It also makes them depressed because they think there is something wrong with them as a person, and that people won't like them or find them attractive.

Clothes also cause problems for a lot of young people in my country. They are very interested in what make of trainers or jeans they wear, and they all want to buy the clothes that are considered the most fashionable. If you haven't got those clothes, people of your age laugh at you. This is a problem for people who haven't got enough money to buy these 'designer' clothes because these clothes are often very expensive. It's a problem for their parents too because they want their children to be happy, but they can't afford these things.

In my opinion, this is all unnecessary. I think that it's much more important what sort of person you are than what you look like. Young people shouldn't worry so much about their appearance; they should enjoy life more while they are young.

▶ **General Training Module: Test B**

Task 1 *(page 197)*

> Dear Sir or Madam,
>
> I visited your museum last Saturday with a couple of friends of mine, who do not speak English very well, and who had their small child with them in a pushchair. I would like to tell you how enjoyable our visit was because of the help given to us by your staff.
>
> When we arrived, there was a long queue at the entrance, but a member of staff saw that we had a small child with us and took us immediately to the front of the queue and into the museum. As we went round the museum, we asked members of staff various questions about the exhibits, and they explained everything very patiently and in a way that my friends could easily understand. They are clearly experienced in this sort of situation and very well trained.
>
> Our visit was a great success, and this is mainly because of your staff. I would be grateful if you could thank them on our behalf for treating us so well and helping to give us a memorable day.
>
> Yours faithfully,
> J. Dowie

Task 2 *(page 198)*

> Most parents want their children to do well in life and so it is understandable that they expect them to be ambitious. A lot of parents who don't have much money and are not at the higher levels of society want their children to do better in life than they did, to have opportunities that they did not have, to have better jobs than they had and to have money to buy things that they could not buy. It is natural for them to think in this way, and therefore it is hard for them to accept it if their children do not have big things in life that they want to achieve.
>
> However, not everyone can be successful in life. Not everyone is clever enough to get a highly-paid job and not everyone is capable of achieving what their parents would regard as success. Some young people would rather be happy and live a relaxed life than spend all their time trying to achieve ambitions that they might not be able to achieve anyway. And lots of people don't find anything that they desperately want to achieve. They are happy to get ordinary jobs, earn a living and enjoy themselves with their friends and family.
>
> In my opinion, it is understandable that a lot of parents want their children to be ambitious, but it is also natural that not all young people are ambitious. Your youth is a time for enjoying yourself, and there is no reason why everyone should have big goals in life. There are more important things.

BRITISH COUNCIL

 idp IELTS AUSTRALIA

 CAMBRIDGE ENGLISH
Language Assessment
Part of the University of Cambridge

S A M P L E
IELTS Listening and Reading Answer Sheet

Centre number:

Pencil must be used to complete this sheet.

Please write your **full name** in CAPITAL letters on the line below:

_____

Then write your six digit Candidate number in the boxes and
shade the number in the grid on the right.

Test date (shade ONE box for the day, ONE box for the month and ONE box for the year):

Day: 01 02 03 04 05 06 07 08 09 10 11 12 13 14 15 16 17 18 19 20 21 22 23 24 25 26 27 28 29 30 31

Month: 01 02 03 04 05 06 07 08 09 10 11 12   **Year** (last 2 digits): 13 14 15 16 17 18 19 20 21

	Listening Listening Listening	Marker use only		Listening Listening Listening	Marker use only
1		✓ 1 ✗	21		✓ 21 ✗
2		✓ 2 ✗	22		✓ 22 ✗
3		✓ 3 ✗	23		✓ 23 ✗
4		✓ 4 ✗	24		✓ 24 ✗
5		✓ 5 ✗	25		✓ 25 ✗
6		✓ 6 ✗	26		✓ 26 ✗
7		✓ 7 ✗	27		✓ 27 ✗
8		✓ 8 ✗	28		✓ 28 ✗
9		✓ 9 ✗	29		✓ 29 ✗
10		✓ 10 ✗	30		✓ 30 ✗
11		✓ 11 ✗	31		✓ 31 ✗
12		✓ 12 ✗	32		✓ 32 ✗
13		✓ 13 ✗	33		✓ 33 ✗
14		✓ 14 ✗	34		✓ 34 ✗
15		✓ 15 ✗	35		✓ 35 ✗
16		✓ 16 ✗	36		✓ 36 ✗
17		✓ 17 ✗	37		✓ 37 ✗
18		✓ 18 ✗	38		✓ 38 ✗
19		✓ 19 ✗	39		✓ 39 ✗
20		✓ 20 ✗	40		✓ 40 ✗

Marker 2 Signature		Marker 1 Signature		Listening Total	

IELTS L-R v1.0

denote Print Limited 0121 520 5100

DP787/394

Please write your **full name** in CAPITAL letters on the line below:

S A M P L E

Please write your Candidate number on the line below:

_____

Please write your three digit language code in the boxes and shade the numbers in the grid on the right.

0 1 2 3 4 5 6 7 8 9
0 1 2 3 4 5 6 7 8 9
0 1 2 3 4 5 6 7 8 9

Are you: Female? ▭   Male? ▭

Reading Reading Reading Reading Reading Reading

Module taken (shade one box):   Academic ▭   General Training ▭

#		Marker use only	#		Marker use only
1		✓ 1 ✗	21		✓ 21 ✗
2		✓ 2 ✗	22		✓ 22 ✗
3		✓ 3 ✗	23		✓ 23 ✗
4		✓ 4 ✗	24		✓ 24 ✗
5		✓ 5 ✗	25		✓ 25 ✗
6		✓ 6 ✗	26		✓ 26 ✗
7		✓ 7 ✗	27		✓ 27 ✗
8		✓ 8 ✗	28		✓ 28 ✗
9		✓ 9 ✗	29		✓ 29 ✗
10		✓ 10 ✗	30		✓ 30 ✗
11		✓ 11 ✗	31		✓ 31 ✗
12		✓ 12 ✗	32		✓ 32 ✗
13		✓ 13 ✗	33		✓ 33 ✗
14		✓ 14 ✗	34		✓ 34 ✗
15		✓ 15 ✗	35		✓ 35 ✗
16		✓ 16 ✗	36		✓ 36 ✗
17		✓ 17 ✗	37		✓ 37 ✗
18		✓ 18 ✗	38		✓ 38 ✗
19		✓ 19 ✗	39		✓ 39 ✗
20		✓ 20 ✗	40		✓ 40 ✗

Marker 2 Signature		Marker 1 Signature		Reading Total

9781285747217